THE HUNGRY BIRD BOOK

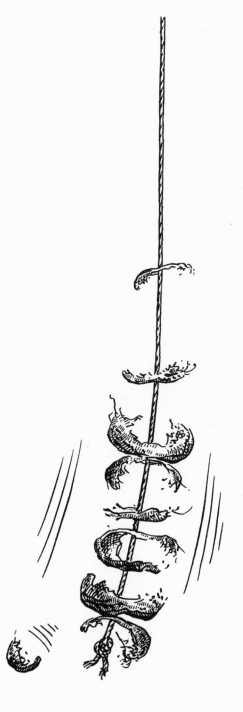

The

ROBERT ARBIB
& TONY SOPER

Hungry Bird Book

Illustrations by Robert Gillmor

TAPLINGER PUBLISHING COMPANY
New York

Published in the United States in 1971 by
TAPLINGER PUBLISHING CO., INC.
New York, New York

International Standard Book Number 0-8008-4020-8
Library of Congress Catalog Card Number 75-122251
Published simultaneously in the Dominion of Canada by
Burns & MacEachern Ltd., Ontario
Printed in the United States of America

Third Printing

Contents

Introduction

In 1965, Tony Soper, an English filmmaker with a love of nature and an eye for beauty, wrote a useful and charming little book about bringing wild birds more closely into our lives, which he called *The Bird Table Book*. It was written for a British audience, about British gardens and the birds that live in them. It was and is an unqualified success.

In adapting and revising *The Bird Table Book* for an audience on our side of the Atlantic, we have tried to retain as much of the easy informality of style and the content of the original as we could. Where possible, we have kept Tony's words, changing only the names of birds, plants, insects and such. Some major revisions and additions were required. The birds we find in our gardens are not the same, although many of them are related to those that haunt British gardens. Our gardens are different in some ways, although under snow a garden in New Jersey might look just like one in Surrey. A garden in Florida, Texas or mid-Ontario, on the other hand, presents new problems. Tony Soper described 65 species of British birds that might be attracted to the garden to feed, bathe or nest. In an area far larger and more diverse, we have described or mentioned 99 species, and the list could have been doubled or tripled if we had included all those species which will on occasion visit the American or Canadian garden, in migration, in winter wanderings or to nest. Our criteria for inclusion were 1) regularly attracted to gardens for food or water set out; 2) nest in boxes, platforms or other spaces provided by man; 3) common somewhere in our area. A common bird such as the American Redstart, for example, would be excluded because although it may nest in the woodlot behind your garden, it does not nest in a habitation provided by you, or come to your feeding tray.

The Hungry Bird Book is thus an Anglo-American effort. It is written to be useful to anyone living in the area served by Roger Tory Peterson's invaluable *A Field Guide to the Birds,* or the American continent roughly east of the 100th meridian, henceforth referred to as "our area."

We trust that Tony—and the birds—approve.

ROBERT ARBIB

Preface

The love of mankind for the garden is as old as civilization—as old as Eden itself—and this fascination holds no great mystery. For in our private garden we can, each in our own way, play God on a little plot of earth, bring forth the fruit of our own imaginations, our own concepts of beauty and tranquillity, harmony and peace. Starting with bare earth or tangled wilderness, we can, through our own labor and our love, bring forth a minor miracle, a paradise of our own planning, filled with all the colors and fragrances in God's own palette, and the songs of birds. Which, to most of us, is all the divinity we will ever need.

For the songs of birds and the flashing of their wings, a special kind of garden is required. It may be part of a rolling expanse of acreage, or a high-walled city yard; whatever its size, it can be made more attractive to birds and attract more birds to it. All that is needed is that we provide sustenance in the form of food and water, shelter against the elements and sites for nests.

Obviously, there are some miracles that even the most devoted gardener cannot perform. He cannot attract nesting waterfowl to the suburban plot without a sizable pond; he cannot attract woodland-breeding species to a city garden surrounded by tall buildings;

he cannot bring birds of dune and saltmarsh to the upland farm; he cannot play host to wild birds *and* footloose cats, or attract much of anything to a tiny terrace on the 23rd story of an apartment house.

This book is written primarily for those with at least some chance of success: the suburbanite or country dweller with a plot of ground big enough to be called, without embarassment, a garden, and one that is not totally impaired by continual disturbance—by human intrusion (small children particularly) or animals—or the proximity of heavy vehicular traffic.

The city dweller is by no means ruled out, although his task is more difficult. One friend of ours has seen from his garden, 20 by 34 feet in the heart of midtown Manhattan, no less than 120 species (mostly migrants) attracted by the oasis of greenery he has provided in the concrete desert. Another, sitting smack athwart a sub-flyway, has listed 247 species in a densely wooded backyard strip exactly 20 feet wide, bordered on both sides by junkyards.

Let it be said at the outset that the bird garden can be a creation of bloom and beauty, but if birds are the primary goal, it may not always meet with the approval of those neighbors who cherish order, regularity of design and textbook maintenance at all times. Birds like lots of cover and tangles, which may mean dense border plantings not always beloved by neighbors, and they like seeds, which means letting flowers (and weeds) go to seed, when the tidy gardener would be tempted to cut, burn and clean. But of course a compromise is possible. Birds will come to a clean garden, if it has all the other desirable features.

For Ren, who puts up with it all:
seed bin on the porch, scrap bags in the kitchen,
camera junk in the bathroom, binoculars at the bedside
and bird books everywhere

1 The Bird Garden

An open, well-kept (but not sterilized) lawn is almost essential to a bird garden. It gives you a clear view, and provides a happy hunting area for birds searching for earthworms, beetles, grubs, ants and all the other small denizens of the "grassroots jungle." And please do not try to kill your worms, especially with a worm-killer containing chlordane. Worms are useful: they aerate and fertilize the soil, and though wormcasts may be unsightly, they consist of fine rich soil. Spread them with a lawn rake or drag a weighted piece of wire netting over them before mowing. In the autumn, don't be too quick to rake up fallen leaves. Worms like leaves (especially willow and cherry) and birds like worms.

The bird garden should have a varied terrain whenever possible, with changes of levels, brushy corners, low dry stone walls—all features which will provide a diversity of insect life and rich foraging areas. Birds live on an incredibly diverse diet of plant life (berries, buds, fruits and seeds) and animal life of the lower orders, and the more variety you provide, the more birds you will attract. Flower beds and neat borders do not offer much of interest, at least during the blooming season (hummingbirds excepted), and an overtidy garden is an unexciting hunting ground. In fact, the less formal, more natural, more "wild" your setting, the more hospitable your bird table.

In northern areas a rock bank, low wall or other sheltered haven in a warm or south-facing part of your garden will be less deeply snow-covered and sooner bare in thaws. The basics: a good lawn. plenty of berry-bearing trees and shrubs for a perimeter and (to provide quiet and seclusion) islands of seed-bearing plants and a reasonable amount of "jungle." With careful and planned planting you can have a garden that is green, attractive and alive with birds year round. And acceptable even in the most manicured of neighborhoods.

Incidentally, if you are buying a new house or having one built, be certain that the builders set the topsoil aside for subsequent replacement before they start crashing about with bulldozers. Builders are all too ready to bury your vital topsoil under tons of useless subsoil, or cart it away altogether, and you will find it is a long uphill grind to produce a fertile garden. And insist that every possible tree consistent with your garden plan be left untouched.

One of the best bird garden boundaries ever devised is the Devon hedgerow, a feature unfamiliar in America and not everywhere feasible. A wide foundation bank with rough stones, with ivy and ferns and wild flowers growing out of it, and topped with a close-planted hedge of hawthorn, multiflora rose, coralberry or high bush cranberry, is a bird paradise. One of the many beauties of a hedgerow is that it provides a variety of food in winter when natural resources are at their lowest ebb. Thrushes, Robins, Mockingbirds and many other birds will eat berry pulp and pass the seeds. Then sparrows and chickadees will eat the seeds as they forage along the base of the hedgerow. Dead leaves and debris shelter hibernating flies and insects, spiders and centipedes, all of which are good for Winter Wrens, chickadees, Hermit Thrushes, Catbirds and towhees. In the hedge itself, some leaves stay attached and provide warmth and cover throughout the winter. The bank harbors yet more grubs and insects, wintering aphids and their eggs, chrysalids and so on.

If you haven't the space to develop a Devon hedgerow, then a dense hedge of holly, pyracantha, bush honeysuckle, viburnum or the other shrubs listed above will do very well indeed. Put a couple of crabapple trees in it; they will provide useful standby food in hard weather.

Generally speaking, it is well to avoid planting coarse thick-leaved evergreens. The rhododendrons and laurels beloved of town park commissions and landscape experts are unpromising bird habitats, taking light from the ground and not offering many insects in return. If you have room, you might plant an isolated cluster of pines, hemlocks or other cone-bearers (or red cedar) in the hope of attracting kinglets, Pine Siskins, crossbills, Red-breasted Nuthatches and many other species. But have *some evergreens* certainly, because they provide autumn and winter cover for roosting birds. A berry-bearing (female) holly will serve a double purpose: food and beauty. Have one tall tree at least, and your Robin, Mockingbird, towhee, thrasher, or oriole will sing from its topmost branch.

If you are lucky enough to have some old fruit trees, keep one or two for the birds. Leave the fruit on them and it will be welcome in winter—shriveled, dried, but still nourishing. Ruffed Grouse, in rural areas, like nothing better than to forage under the apple trees.

Berry-bearing trees and shrubs—a selected list

AMERICAN HOLLY. *Ilex opaca.* This is our familiar "Christmas Holly," whose bright scarlet berries are favored by many species of birds from thrushes and Mockingbirds to Cedar Waxwings and Cardinals. It is hardy from Massachusetts south along the east coast. It will thrive in poor or sandy soil and in deep shade. Only the females bear fruit, but a male must be planted nearby for fertilization. Perhaps even more attractive, because of its shinier, darker foliage and brighter berries is the ENGLISH HOLLY, *Ilex aquifolium.* Two recommended varieties are Golden King (small: to 10 feet) a good berry producer, and Madame Briot (to 18 feet) with golden berries. Many other varieties are available. Hollies make fine hedge or border plantings and are handsome as specimen trees.

AUTUMN OLIVE. *Elaeagnus umbellata.* In the U.S., one of the newer favorites among birdfeeding trees, bearing in autumn masses of yellowish-pink berries attractive to scores of species. Handsome silvergreen foliage on drooping branches; grows in poor, sandy soil and near salt water. Perhaps too irregular in growth for the smaller garden, but excellent as a shelter belt hedge or in clusters. Considered by some authorities as the finest of all winter-fruit trees for birds. Hardy in the far north. Plant both males and females.

RED MULBERRY. *Morus rubra.* A mulberry in fruit is one of the most irresistible of all trees to birds. In late June and July it will swarm with a frantic concourse of Robins, Catbirds, orioles and many other species, gorging themselves on the blackberry-like fruit. The mulberry is a highly ornamental tree with a crown spreading from a short trunk. It may reach 70 feet in southern forests, but is normally under 50 feet in height. Hardy from Massachusetts and Nebraska south. The exotic WHITE MULBERRY, *Morus alba,* is equally attractive to birds, but less resistant to extremes of heat and cold.

HAWTHORNS. *Crataegus sp.* Ornamental small flowering trees, thorny, with red or yellow fruit favored by birds of many species. Makes an excellent boy-proof hedge. Autumn foliage is flamboyant. Among the more attractive varieties (to birds) both for nest sites and winter fare are WHITE HAWTHORN, *C. coccinea,* SCARLET HAWTHORN, *C. mollis,* WASHINGTON THORN, *C. phaenopyrum* and many horticultural varieties of the ENGLISH and NEWCASTLE THORN, *C. crus-galli.* In the south, a favored variety is the PARSLEY HAWTHORN, *C. spathulata,* ideal for Texas, Oklahoma and southern states.

VIBURNUMS. *Viburnum sp.* A large family of fruit-bearing shrubs or small trees, many of them ornamental. Their fruits last well into the winter and are attractive to many species of songbirds, from Brown Thrasher and thrushes to Red-eyed Vireo and cuckoos. Among the preferred species are MAPLE-LEAF VIBURNUM, *V. acerifolium,* EUROPEAN CRANBERRY BUSH, *V. opulus,* HIGHBUSH CRANBERRY, *V. trilobum,* SIEBOLD VIBURNUM, *V. sieboldi,* NANNYBERRY, *V. lentago* and ARROWWOOD, *V. dentatum.*

CHERRY. *Prunus sp.* A cherry tree in one's garden is a guarantee of hosts of bird visitors; in fruiting season (July to September) the activity is continuous. For gardens, the CHOKECHERRY, *P. virginia,* is most compact. The BLACK CHERRY, *P. serotina,* almost a weed tree in the East, is rather short-lived and messy, but a bird magnet. WILD RED CHERRY, *P. pensylvanica,* is also favored by birds. *P. maritima,* the BEACH PLUM, thrives in sandy soil and coastal areas of the Northeast.

AMERICAN ELDER. *Sambucus pubens.* ELDERBERRY. *Sambucus canadensis.* Two of our prize bird food producers, with masses of purple-black fruit in late summer and fall. Devoured by almost all songbirds. Good cover shrubs, growing to 12 feet, liking wet soil, in shade or sun and hardy into Canada. (Make a good country wine.)

DOGWOOD. *Cornus sp.* The glory of the American woodland, and perhaps America's favorite flowering tree, although the birds eat its bitter scarlet fruit as a last resort. The native WHITE DOGWOOD, *Cornus florida,* is now sold in "improved" strains, including *xanthocarpus,* which bears yellow fruit. Among attractive species are *Cornus kousa,* JAPANESE FLOWERING DOG-WOOD (pink fruit), ALTERNATE-LEAVED DOGWOOD, *C. alternifolia,* with purple fruit, OSIER DOGWOOD, *C. stolonifera,* SILKY DOGWOOD, *C. amomum,* and SIBERIAN DOG-WOOD, *C. alba sibirica.*

Evergreens that should be in every bird garden, for cover, nesting sites or food: YEW, *Taxus baccata,* CANADIAN HEMLOCK, *Tsuga canadensis,* WHITE PINE, *Pinus strobus,* and RED CEDAR, *Juniperus virginiana.*

Bush plants

HIGHBUSH BLUEBERRY. *Vaccinium corymbosum.* The delicious pie fillers are also gobbled up by the birds and are gone almost before they ripen. The blueberry provides cover and nesting sites for Chipping and Song Sparrows. If you want pie instead of birds, you must cover the ripening berries.

WILD BLACKBERRY. *Rubus alleghaniensis.* A wonderful bird provider, needs cultivation and cutting back for heaviest bearing. Will spread into a thick tangle if not controlled, in which Cardinal, Catbird, thrasher and Song Sparrow will nest.

POKEBERRY. *Phytolacca americana.* A weed that often seeds itself from bird droppings, producing juicy purple berries irresistible to thrushes and many other species.

Fox Grape. *Vitis labrusca* (early). Difficult to control for the small garden, but a grape tangle is a fine bird food and cover vine. Also good: FROST GRAPE, *V. vulpina* (late).

Tartarian Honeysuckle. *Lonicera tatarica.* There are a number of ornamental bush honeysuckles, beloved by birds for nesting and their red midsummer berries. This one is spring fruiting and one of the best. Also: MORROW'S HONEYSUCKLE, *L. morrowi,* and BLUE-LEAF HONEYSUCKLE, *L. korolkowi.* In southern areas, TRUMPET HONEYSUCKLE, *L. sempervirens and* HALL'S HONEYSUCKLE, *L. japonica halliana,* are recommended.

Bayberry. Wax Myrtle. *Myrica pensylvanica, M. cerifera.* An aromatic, almost evergreen dense shrub or tree, much favored by warblers and many other songbirds for its waxy, gray berries. Grows in any soil, including pure sand. Needs sunlight.

Multiflora Rose. *Rosa multiflora.* Excellent for cover, for nesting and for winter-lingering food. One of the finest live fences and hedges. Takes to almost any well-drained soil. But it needs room!

The list could be expanded many times. Among other fine food providers are: FIRETHORN, *Pyracantha sp.*; CHOKEBERRY, *Aronia arbutifolia*; INKBERRY, *Ilex glabra*; JAPANESE BARBERRY, *Berberis thunbergi;* GREENBRIER or CATBRIER, *Smilax sp.* Good ground covers include: BEARBERRY, *Arctostaphylos uva-ursi* (northern areas); BUNCHBERRY, *Cornus canadensis;* PARTRIDGEBERRY, *Mitchella repens* (rich soils); WINTERGREEN, *Gaultheria procumbens.* None of these will survive in bright sunlight.

Should your garden have flowers (and it should), you might let them go to seed for an additional source of bird food. Here are some of the seedbearers your birds will welcome: CHINESE ASTER, *Callistephus chinensis;* BACHELOR BUTTON, *Centaurea cyanus;* BELLFLOWER, *Campanula medium;* BLACK-EYED SUSAN, *Rudbeckia laciniata;* CALIFORNIA POPPY, *Eschscholtzia californica;* CHRYSANTHEMUM, *Chrysanthemum sp.;* COLUMBINE, *Aquilegia, sp.;* COSMOS, *Cosmos bipinnatus;* FORGET-ME-NOT, *Myosotis sp.;* LOVE-LIES-BLEEDING, *Amaranthus caudatus;* MARIGOLD, *Tagetes sp.;* PETUNIA, *Petunia hybrida;* PRINCE'S FEATHER, *Amaranthus hypochondriacus;* SCABIOUS, *Scabiosa caucasica;* SNAPDRAGON, *An-*

tirrhinum majus; SUNFLOWER, *Helianthus anuus;* SWEET
WILLIAM, *Dianthus barbatus;* VERVAIN, *Verbena sp.;* ZIN-
NIA, *Zinnia elegans.*

2 Water

Although there are some species, even whole families of birds that can apparently live out their lives without drinking water, most of our garden birds will die within a few days without it. Although birds do not sweat, they lose water both by respiration and excretion and must make up the loss. Some they will make up from the flesh of berries or insect food and the rest from drinking. Tree-living species may sip from foliage after rain, but most birds will visit ponds and streams. Some will fill their bills, then raise their heads to let water run down their throats; some will keep their bills in the water; some will sip from the surface of the water as they fly past. Swifts and swallows even bathe in flight, dipping under with a quick splash as they go by.

Most birds also need water to help with the constant problem of keeping their plumage in order. Quite apart from the fact that feathers are a vital part of their flying apparatus, plumage acts as an insulator and helps to regulate body temperature. To be fully efficient, the feathers must be kept in good condition, and feather maintenance looms large in a bird's life. Bathing is the first move in a complicated sequence of events.

The object of the bath is to wet the plumage without actually soaking it. Birds will sometimes bathe in light rain, but if they are caught out in a heavy downpour, they will hunch up into a special position, reaching upwards and tightening their feathers so that the rain pours off quickly.

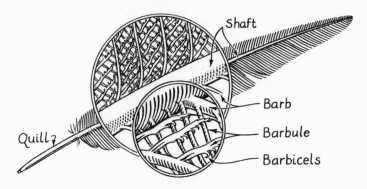

After the bath the bird will shake itself and begin "oiling." With the tail twisted to one side, it will reach down with its bill to collect fatty oil from its preen gland. Then, very carefully, it will rub the oil into the feathers all over the body. The difficult stage

Mockingbird scratching and oiling

comes when it wants to oil its head. To do this it will use a foot, first oiling the foot and then scratching the head. Next comes the preening session, when the bird will nibble and smooth out all its feathers. This may take a long time, and afterwards the bird will stretch and settle itself until its plumage is in full flying and insulating order.

Unless you are lucky enough to have a stream or pond in your garden, you will have to provide water in some form or another. The bird bath is the obvious answer, although it is not the best. However, if you are short of space, it will suffice. The simplest version is an upturned garbage can lid, supported by three bricks or sunk into the ground, although if you sink it, you will have more trouble keeping it ice-free in winter.

If you balk at introducing garbage can lids into your garden, use any similarly shaped shallow bowl, but beware of those plastic, so-called bird baths which may have a slippery slope leading to a cavernous well. Garden supply or garden ornament stores today stock a multitude of well-designed bird baths: look for a wide, shallow bowl with a low lip for a bird perch. We prefer cast stone in natural or rustic colors. At all costs avoid bird baths or fountains with lead sheet linings; lead poisoning of your birds may result.

Whatever kind of bowl or bowls you use, put them in sunshine and within reasonable range of cover and safety, but not so close that a cat may lie in ambush. A point to remember is that birds get rather excited and preoccupied about their bathing and therefore are more vulnerable than at other times.

Try to avoid letting the bath go dry, although this may mean constant refilling in hot weather. It is especially important to keep it ice-free in winter. If the bowl is breakable, put a chunk of softwood into it so that when the water freezes the strain will be taken by the wood and not the bowl. Occasionally, a small bird will actually crack a very thin layer of ice to drink, but this only shows how badly it needs water.

Available commercially are immersion heaters designed to keep bird baths permanently ice-free. Metal heaters are more reliable than those with glass-enclosed heating elements which are often used in photographic darkrooms and aquariums. Be sure that the wiring is suitable for the outdoors and that all connections are waterproof; then there will be no danger to the birds. One such heater is sold by Smith-Gates Corporation, Farmington, Connecticut, but the two we have tried have not been totally satisfactory. (They must be immersed two inches below the surface, which means a too-deep bowl. And if the birds lower the water level, exposing the heater, it can overheat and burn out.)

Especially attractive to birds is water that shows a little motion, a steady drip, trickle or fine-spray fountain. It will increase your bird bath traffic many times over! Perhaps the simplest device is a water bucket or pail suspended well over the bath, with a tiny nail hole punched in the bottom. (Don't overestimate the size of hole that will result in a steady drip. Make it very small at first; you can always enlarge it.) A more attractive and permanent trickle can be created by attaching with a readily-available coupling, a ¼-inch copper or plastic tubing to a hose bibb, rigged to trickle into bath or pool. (See the illustration below). An adjustable fountain spray that attaches to a garden hose is sold

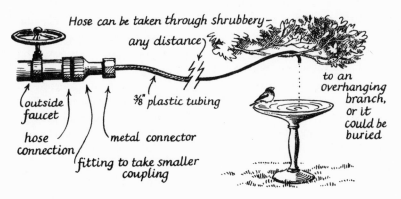

Hose can be taken through shrubbery— any distance

⅜" plastic tubing

outside faucet

hose connection

fitting to take smaller coupling

metal connector

to an overhanging branch, or it could be buried

by Beverly Specialties, Box 9, Riverside, Illinois. Recirculating fountain equipment is not suitable; bathing birds scatter water in every direction and your bath will need constant refilling. If you do improve the bath with running water, it should be set firmly on a well-drained base, crushed rock or gravel all around. Or be prepared for mud.

Do not use glycerine or anti-freeze of any kind to keep water ice-free. These chemicals will cause havoc with a bird's feathers at a time when they should be in first-class condition to keep out the cold. People sometimes ask why birds bathe so much in freezing weather and the answer must now be obvious. To keep warm, the feathers must be efficient, and to have efficient feathers the bird must go through the preening ritual, which starts with a bath.

Sketches of a
young Robin
preening
after bathing

While a bird bath will serve its purpose quite adequately, a properly stocked and regulated pool with oxygenating plants and fish is infinitely preferable and much more rewarding. The water should be very shallow, but if you are going to make a special pond, and a sizable one, you may want to have a deeper section in which to raise fish in the hope of attracting kingfishers and herons. Design the pond so that there is a gently-shelving shallow area leading to the main depth of three feet or more. And provide a gently-sloping approach to the shallow area so that small mammals, rabbits and such, can come to drink and bathe (and get out again).

First, prepare your pit and line it with sand or gravel. Some small ponds can be lined with polyethylene or polyvinyl sheeting and will require no other waterproofing. But if concrete is used to make the job more permanent, it should be six inches thick and the mix made of one part cement, two parts sharp sand, and three parts washed gravel. Use just enough water to make a stiff (not sloppy) mix. When it is dry, paint it or spray it with a water sealer, not only to seal the chemical elements and avoid poisoning your wildlife, but to improve the waterproofing. When your concrete is set and sealed, put several inches of good soil in the bottom for your plants. Do your planting before you fill your pond. (You may have to anchor some of your plants in the soil with stones.) Fill carefully, either through a fine watering nozzle or by watering into a bowl or pan, letting the water slowly pour over the edges. The idea is to keep from churning the soil up and dislodging your plants.

It is essential to put in some oxygenating plants to absorb the carbon dioxide produced by all the water creatures which will colonize your pool. These plants are vital if you wish to keep a healthy, smell-free pool. Get pest-free specimens from nurseries or aquarium supply houses. The following plants are recommended, all of which are oxygenating and will grow in a few inches of soil under water:

DUCK POTATO. *Sagittaria heterophylla, S. cuneata, S. latifolia, S. graminea,* and *S. platyphylla.* This plant will also absorb excreta from wildlife, as manure.

ARROWLEAF. ARROW ARUM. *Peltandra virginica.*

COONTAIL. *Ceratophyllum demersum.* Floating, needs no planting. in shade.

COMMON DUCKWEED. *Lemna minor.* Floating plant, grows best
SAGO PONDWEED. *Potamogeton pectinatus.* One of several valuable pondweeds. Plant roots in late summer or fall.

Callitriche autumnalis. Retains oxygenating properties through the winter.

WATER VIOLET. *Hottonia palustris.*

QUILLWORT. *Isoetes lacustris.* An excellent fish food.

Use no lead in anchoring the plants in their soil. If there is enough room, have a small island in the middle of the pond, but, in any case, fix a couple of small sticks in such a way that small birds can hang on them while they drink. The most simple method is to submerge a flowerpot upside down in the water and poke a stick through the hole.

In a week or so, when the plants have taken hold and the water has cleared, introduce some fish. Goldfish if you like, but why not good native species like minnows? Any of these will deal with the mosquito and gnat larvae which will try to breed in the pool.

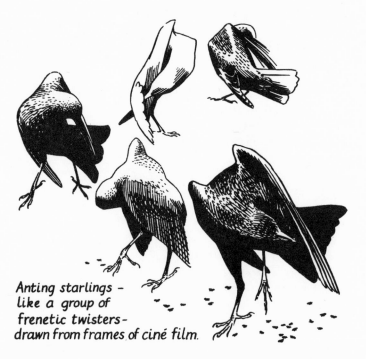

*Anting starlings –
like a group of
frenetic twisters –
drawn from frames of ciné film.*

There are plenty of other creatures you can introduce, such as frogs, water striders, water beetles, backswimmers and such. You will find that the finished product will give you as much pond-watching pleasure as it does the birds, and if one day a heron comes and eats your fish, you must grin and bear it and restock your pond.

Unless your garden is on sandy ground, you may wish to provide a dust bath to help sparrows and other small birds get rid of their parasites. The dusting place should be in sunlight and near cover, and can consist merely of a few square feet of powdery sand, earth and ash to a depth of a few inches. Sprinkle the dust bath with an aerosol insecticide now and then (no DDT or chlorinated hydrocarbons, please) for the common good. Birds will also sun bathe, smoke bathe, and even anoint themselves with ants, which practice apparently applies formic acid or other natural mite killer to the birds' skin.

3 Nest Sites and Bird Boxes

Your bird visitors are now well-fed and watered, and the next move is to improve their nesting facilities. By their nature, houses, outbuildings and gardens provide dozens of potential nesting sites, although in these tidy-minded days we tend to build with fewer holes and corners. But very often we can turn an uninviting building into a highly desirable residence for birds with a minimum of effort. Once again we must bear in mind that different birds have different requirements, and that while a chickadee or House Wren will choose a secret place, entered by what seems like an impossibly narrow hole, a swan will build a great mound of a nest and sit in state for all to see (usually, however, in an inaccessible spot on an island or in a marsh).

We can divide birds roughly and unscientifically into those which nest in cavities and those which do not. Chickadees, nuthatches and woodpeckers are hole nesters, while warblers, blackbirds and thrushes live on the open plan. All birds, no matter what type of nest they build, need protection from their enemies and shelter from the elements if they are to thrive, so many of them build in cover of some kind. Birds which nest completely in the open, such as shorebirds, terns and nighthawks have young which are well developed when hatched—or at least provided with fluffy down.

NATURAL NEST SITES. Since most of our garden birds require cover, a hedge, thicket, or strip of untouched brush will provide excellent nesting ground for a number of species. A good holly, privet, hawthorn, hemlock or multiflora rose hedge contains dozens of likely building sites and offers shelter, concealment and a multitude of escape routes for small birds. It is important that there should be plenty of forks in the branches, to provide underpinning for the first nest twigs. By judicious pruning at various heights you can often turn an unpromising hedge into an inviting nest site. Prune your hedges early in spring or autumn, leaving them undisturbed during the breeding season. While pruning fruit trees, make a crotch site here and there in the body of the tree, in the hope of attracting a Robin, a Least Flycatcher or a Kingbird.

The berry-bearing shrubs often serve as nesting areas in spring: if you have blackberries, you may find that they harbor Catbirds or thrashers. Honeysuckle seems to have a special attraction for Catbirds, barberry for Chipping Sparrows. Following are some of the garden-nesting species that may make their homes in your hedges, thickets and shrubby borders:

Mockingbird	Yellow Warbler	American Goldfinch
Brown Thrasher	Yellowthroat	Rufous-sided Towhee
Catbird	Yellow-breasted Chat	Chipping Sparrow
White-eyed Vireo	Cardinal	Song Sparrow
	Purple Finch	

In the South (Florida) add

> Gray Kingbird   Boat-tailed Grackle
> Scrub Jay   Painted Bunting

A dense conifer hedge may attract nesting

> Mourning Dove   House Finch (in its range)
> Blue Jay   Chipping Sparrow
> Purple Finch

Once a bird has chosen its nest site, leave it (or them) to get on with the job. Don't try to help it with the construction, and don't "improve" the situation or it may desert. Don't fuss with it!

If you have a larger garden, or a place with "estate" proportions, you will add a host of other nesting species depending on the habitat you provide: woodland-nesting species such as woodpeckers, crows, the thrushes, vireos, warblers, Ovenbird, Scarlet Tanager, Rose-breasted Grosbeak, with Indigo Buntings around the edges. If you have open fields or meadows you may enjoy the company of such species as Killdeer, Bobolink, meadowlark, Grasshopper Sparrow, Vesper Sparrow, and Field Sparrow, and even perhaps such comparative rarities as Upland Plover, Short-billed Marsh Wren, and Henslow's Sparrow. If you have a pond, an island in the center may reward you with a nesting pair of Canada Geese. If you are lucky enough to have plenty of water, plant it with those aquatics listed above, plus PICKERELWEED, *Pontederia cordata* (chiefly in the eastern states); SMARTWEEDS, *Polygonum sp.;* WATERCRESS, *Sisymbrium nasturtium-aquaticum* (for cool, clean waters in northern areas); WILD CELERY, *Vallisineria spiralis,* for north-eastern and north central areas, in waters with a slow current; WILD RICE, *Zizania aquatica,* in shallow waters; and RUSHES, *Scirpus americana* and *S. acutus.* With aquatics and edge plantings such as these, you increase your chances of attracting such breeding birds as Pied-billed Grebe, Virginia Rail, Blue-winged Teal, Sora Rail, Common Gallinule, American Coot, Long-billed Marsh Wren, and Red-winged Blackbird.

Now for the hole nesters. Naturally, they will prefer tree holes, and it may be that you already have some old trees—fruit trees, perhaps—which may have begun to decay in a manner attractive to birds. If not, you might consider introducing some holes into a decaying tree with brace and bit. Start some promising holes about 1¼-inches in diameter, and a Downy or Hairy Woodpecker may finish the job. If the woodpecker gives up, a nuthatch or chickadee (especially in a gray birch) may finish the job. Or you might try importing an old tree trunk, complete with holes, and setting it up in a secluded spot. At worst, you will end up with a pair of Starlings. Although they are usually considered nest site grabbers and pests, Starlings are useful in helping to control Japanese beetle grubs and other lawn-damaging grubs, and they are entertaining vocalists with a mimic talent.

Making and enlarging holes is fun, and when you have finished working on trees, you might turn your attention to the walls of

your house or outbuildings. Quite often it is possible to enlarge natural cracks so that there is the inch and an eighth necessary for a House Wren, Carolina Wren or Bewick's Wren to squeeze through. We are not suggesting that you tear your house apart for a few birds, but you will find plenty of likely and safe places if you look around, armed with a strong auger or wrecking bar. If your barn or garage is suitably situated, try drilling some discreet 1¼-inch holes in the doors—or better still—keep the doors wide open in breeding season. Barn Swallows may colonize. An open piece of fibrous insulation material, such as that used on heating system ducts, provides nesting fluff very attractive to swallows.

The height of holes and cavities is not too vital, although from five to ten feet is probably ideal. Or try a variety of heights from four feet up to twenty. With a desirable site, birds will not be too choosy. Robins have nested at ground level and chickadees as high as 30 feet, although this is unusual. The holes, however, should be in a sheltered position and facing somewhere within an arc from north to southeast. Hot sun is bad, and so is an entrance facing a cold wind.

An old garden shed is an asset to cherish, and if you develop it a little, it may become a thriving bird slum in no time at all. Shelves around the walls and under the roof at different heights could provide homes for swallows. The upper walls, if there is a high window, might even attract Chimney Swifts or a Barn Owl. A bundle of pea sticks in a corner may make a home for a House Wren or Carolina Wren. Leave an old tweed coat hanging up with a wide pocket gaping open for a Carolina Wren. Keep the floor clean, however, to discourage rats. If necessary, put a rat trap tunnel against the walls, but see that it does not let in light and attract ground birds. Make sure there is a good entrance somewhere, in case a bird is locked in by mistake.

On the outside of the shed grow a jungle of creeping ivy or honeysuckle for your Catbird or Song Sparrow. Try importing a brushwood bundle and lean it against an outside wall, with a tempting nesting cavity in the middle. Lastly, lean an old plank against the dampest, darkest wall to make a haven for snails and farm them on behalf of the thrushes.

MAN-MADE NEST SITES. There are good historical precedents for putting up bird houses (Noah must have had a dovecote on top of the ark). In Roman times there was a thriving pigeon-raising "fancy" with rooftop pigeon towns. Columbaria of different architectural styles spread from Rome through Europe and to Britain, and thence to the New World. The custom declined somewhat in this century, but the tradition still flourishes, with thousands of lofts or cotes dedicated to raising pigeons for food and for the sport of pigeon racing.

The provision of nests for wild birds has an equally early origin. The first white settlers in America discovered Indian villages often graced with trees or tall poles festooned with gourds placed there for Purple Martins. Today we can still attract the lovely martins with gourds or with multiple-apartment houses set on poles.

While it has often been written that upwards of fifty species of North American birds will nest in man-provided dwellings, the list of regular tenants of such housing is much shorter. Here are the species in our area that one may hope for with some optimism, remembering that even with this short list, conditions of climate, cover, habitat and topography must be favorable. Chapter six will present the full list of possibilities: Wood Duck, Sparrow Hawk, Screech Owl, Flicker, Hairy Woodpecker, Downy Woodpecker, Crested Flycatcher, Tree Swallow, Barn Swallow, Purple Martin, chickadee (three species), House Wren, Carolina Wren, Bewick's Wren, Bluebird, plus Starling and House Sparrow.

Phoebes and Robins will use nesting platforms in certain situations. In very restricted locations, such species as Osprey may respond to the provision of nesting platforms on poles: they are scarcely garden birds! In the widening area in the eastern U.S.

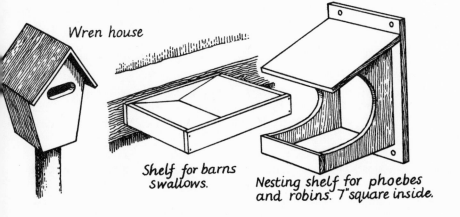

Wren house

Shelf for barns swallows.

Nesting shelf for phoebes and robins. 7" square inside.

where the House Finch has become established, an occasional man-made structure is used. A pair nested quite comfortably in a hanging basket of fuchsia on our front porch, and a recent birdwatcher's convention on Long Island was entertained by a pair nesting inside a functioning ornamental lantern on the hotel terrace—just a few yards from the surf. In a restricted area around St. Louis, Missouri, the European Tree Sparrow uses nest boxes.

Other birds that use man-made structures, but not nesting boxes, include the Common Nighthawk, Rough-winged Swallow, Cliff Swallow and Chimney Swift. Nighthawks often nest on the flat asphalt roofs of commercial buildings and apartment houses if the surface is rough (pebbly) and dry. The Peregrine Falcon has been known to nest on the ledges of city skyscrapers, but alas, that may never happen again. There are no more breeding peregrines in eastern North America.

There are two types of bird houses: an enclosed space with a small entrance hole, and a tray or ledge with or without sides and roof. Garden supply stores, Audubon Society service departments, mail order specialty catalogs and a host of manufacturers offer bird houses of enormous variety, many at reasonable prices.

Audubon magazine and other journals feature much advertising for bird houses and feeding equipment, or you may prefer to make your own; there is an extra satisfaction in seeing birds take over a house you have built (or your child has built) with your own hands. The method of construction will be discussed here in general terms, since the type of house and the critical size entrance for each species will be found in the notes in Chapter 6. The nest hole information that most people want to know first is what size entrance excludes Starlings and House Sparrows. The answer is 1⅛-inches. But remember that birds like Robins and Phoebes live on the open plan and need more shelter than house. So make boxes of both types.

Although it may seem at first sight that the "rustic" type of bird house will be most suitable, the plain finished wood type is probably preferable; the birds certainly do not seem to mind one way or the other, so the main criteria are construction and amenity. The plain, square, "standard" types are undoubtedly easiest to make, and they look most attractive. The rustic boxes are usually made with birch or oak bark. If they are to be attached to the same species of tree, there is no objection, but this is not usually the case. Birch boxes attached to elm trees provide a rather unhappy and unnatural contrast. Perhaps there is some case for using rustic boxes when it is important that they should not be too easily discovered—in public places, for instance—but this is, in our view, a weak one. Small boys on the warpath will discover either type in no time, and if this is a danger, the boxes should be fixed high, not less than ten feet.

The boxes should be made of ¾-inch wood, which will stand up to weathering for a reasonable time and be thick enough to insulate the interior from violent temperature changes. Hardwood is most suitable as it is more resistant to weather than softwood. Redwood is probably the best; seasoned oak is also fine. Of the softwoods, cedar is quite satisfactory and weathers well. It is important that the house should not warp and so allow wind and rain to attack the nestlings. One side should be removable for cleaning purposes, but make sure that it fits firmly in position when in use, and that there is no danger of it falling out and exposing the nest to predators. It is important that the roof be fixed and preferably unhinged so the house is as waterproof as

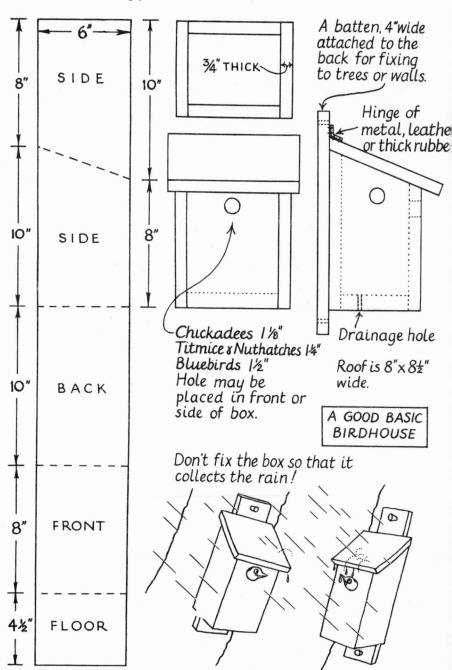

6"

SIDE

8"

10"

3/4" THICK

SIDE

10"

8"

A batten, 4" wide attached to the back for fixing to trees or walls.

Hinge of metal, leather or thick rubber

BACK

10"

Chickadees 1⅛"
Titmice & Nuthatches 1¼"
Bluebirds 1½"
Hole may be placed in front or side of box.

Drainage hole

Roof is 8" x 8½" wide.

A GOOD BASIC BIRDHOUSE

FRONT

8"

Don't fix the box so that it collects the rain!

FLOOR

4½"

possible. Seal the seams with a good commercial caulking compound before you finally nail or screw the pieces together. Rain kills many nestlings in natural nest sites, and we should take particular care to exclude it when we invite birds to use the houses we provide. The entrance hole should be near the top; otherwise, a cat may be able to fish the young birds out, or they may be seen by other predators when they stretch up to beg for food. The inside floor measurements must allow birds plenty of room to stretch their growing wings. Make a couple of drainage holes in the floor, and two or three ¼-inch holes on each side under the roof for cross ventilation.

Ideally, the nestboxes should be fixed in position in October or November. This gives them a chance to weather into their surroundings, and gives their potential tenants (if permanent residents) plenty of time to get used to them and explore their possibilities. It may well be that during the winter some of them will be used for roosting. During the hard winter of 1961-2 in England, there was one almost incredible report of a chickadee box being occupied by no less than fifty wrens, all huddling together for warmth at night. Bird houses, of course, can be put up at any

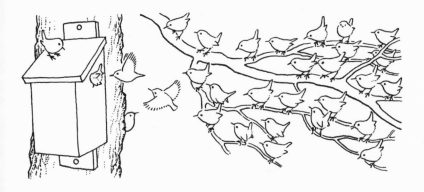

time in the winter, but if you are hoping that they will be occupied in their first spring, they ought to be up by the end of March in northern areas, and by the end of January in the south. However, better late than not at all.

Houses for Purple Martins, of course, follow quite special rules, since the lovely martin is a gregarious fellow and prefers an apartment house built to his own specifications and preferred location. His house should be on a pole 15 to 20 feet above the ground, hinged at the base, as shown in the illustration below, for early spring cleaning. It should be set out in the open, away from overhanging or even shorter foliage (so that he can glide and swoop about without hindrance), and if possible be close to open water, either salt or fresh. Plans for a simple martin house are shown

Martin house

15 - 20 feet
above ground

below. Houses of more than one story should come apart for cleaning. Martins will readily accept houses that are painted; perhaps white, the coolest color, is best. Acceptable martin houses of attractive design in both metal and wood are available wherever

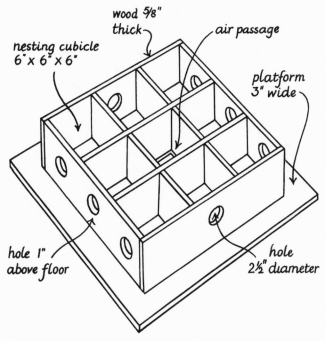

wood ⅝" thick

air passage

nesting cubicle 6" x 6" x 6"

platform 3" wide

hole 1" above floor

hole 2½" diameter

Construction of one floor of Martin house

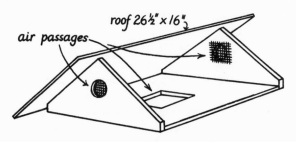

roof 26½" x 16"

air passages

Ventilation in Martin house roof

other bird houses are sold; a number are advertised. Be certain before you order that the inner dimensions of the cells, the entrance diameter and height above the floor are all close to the ideal listed on page 29.

For single bird houses, the direction of the entrance will vary according to the prevailing springtime winds in your area (not directly in line with it), but other factors being equal, a southerly entrance is perhaps used more often. The house location should not be thickly sheltered or darkened by foliage, and the adult birds must have a clear flight path to and from the nest. In fact, the entrance hole must be far enough from its base wall or tree trunk to allow the incoming bird to have fully stretched wings until the last moment before landing. Don't have a landing perch attached to the house: this may provide a cat or squirrel with a good hold for extracting the nestlings. If you want a perch for photographic purposes, put it several feet away. The birds will probably be happy to use it as a staging post.

The house should be fastened in such a way that the top of the entrance hole is inclined outwards to exclude rain, and it should be secured to its anchorage by means of a batten, so that it does not become waterlogged where attached to the wall or tree trunk. It is important to fasten the house securely. An individual pole for each house is probably the safest and best mount of all, although not as attractive as a natural location. But pole-mounted boxes can be further protected from marauding cats and squirrels by a metal cuff or cone on the pole, as shown on page 31.

Do not put up too many houses too close together. Like some of us, some birds prefer to keep their distance from each other. Many species with a strong territorial instinct like to "own" their plot, but fortunately, as a rule, do not object to members of other species living nearby. Thus Robins, which have a strong territorial behavior pattern, will not object to Catbirds as close neighbors, but will fight off other encroaching Robins. It is difficult to say how many houses should be erected, because so many factors are involved, but if you have a large area, it is worth trying a dozen to the acre (for Wood Duck they should be at least 50 yards apart), more if the area is drastically lacking in natural nesting sites. Put up ten closed boxes to one open platform. If there are good natural or semi-natural sites available, it may be that your

Anti-Squirrel
cuff around
birdhouse or
feeder pole

houses will be ignored altogether. On the other hand, you may find birds inspecting, "buying" and starting nest construction within a week.

To make your bird houses even more attractive to passerines, you might try lining the bottoms with a thin layer of moss or straw. If you are hoping for a woodpecker, try priming the box with a sprinkling or more of sawdust or woodshavings, and, as an appetizer, a few beetles and grubs. In early spring, when birds are beginning to build, they will search everywhere for nesting materials. Orioles will take brightly colored lengths of knitting wool, wrens will take horsehair, and many other species will use man-made materials where available.

Straw, feathers, dog or cat combings, rabbit fur, absorbent cotton, cotton threads, loose wool and knitting yarns, kapok and even synthetic fiber-fill material are all grist for their mill. Stuff them into open mesh bags, hanging one from the bird table or a branch, and pegging the other to the ground for ground-feeders. There is nothing more charming than an incubating bird surrounded by a delicate web of colored cottons. The quantity of material used for most cup nests is startling: a naturalist once took a sparrow's nest to pieces and found that it consisted of 1,282 separate items, which included 1,063 pieces of dead grass, 126 strips of bark, 15 pieces of paper, 10 pieces of cellophane, 13 pieces of tissue, 25 pieces of cotton thread, 28 wild bird feathers, one piece of string and a cotton bandage.

Woodpeckers or squirrels may "improve" a bird house, and in one case, a gray squirrel was reported to have enlarged a small hole to 2½-inches in diameter. Do not worry too much about a bird house that gets the woodpecker treatment; a nuthatch may come along and plaster the edges of the hole to suit its own requirements, or a Starling may settle in it. In any case, the house will be useful as a winter roost. Never alter the position of a house

after a bird has adopted it, and never disturb the birds while they are incubating. You will often hear people speak of the tame-

ness of incubating birds; the truth is that the incubating and particularly the brooding instinct is stronger than the bird's terror
of being close to a human being. The bird's nest should be respected
and we should neither fuss nor photograph without good reason.

When, at last, your bird house becomes a noisy, struggling mud-
dle of baby birds, try to contain yourself and do not peer in too
often. Once a day is the absolute maximum, and then you should
make sure that no adult bird is at home. Nothing disconcerts a
wild bird quite as much as the sudden appearance of a vast human
face three inches away. If your house contains a nuthatch, do
not open it at all, as it is more than likely that the loosely made
nest will fall out with all its contents.

All birds are attacked by parasites such as fleas, lice and bird
flies, so after the young have flown, the bird house should be
cleaned out and given a dose of bug-killer. If you now prime
the de-loused house with a thin layer of moss, it will perhaps serve
for a second brood or be ready later on for a winter roosting
place. If the first nesting was unsuccessful, however, you should
leave the nest strictly alone, since in many cases the adult birds
will begin at once on a replacement brood.

Recommended reading:

Cohen, E. and Campbell, B., *Nestboxes*. British Trust for Ornithology, Field Guide No. 3. (Oxford: Potter Press), 1952.

Kalmbach, E. R. and McAtee, W. L., *Homes for Birds*. U. S.
Dept. Int. Conservation Bulletin No. 14, 1957.

Perry, L. D. and Slepicka, F., *Bird Houses*. (Peoria, Ill.: Chas.
A. Bennett Co.), 1955.

McElroy, T. P., Jr., *The New Handbook of Attracting Birds*.
(New York: Alfred Knopf), 1960.

4 The Bird Table

Having produced a garden full of food plants, nesting sites, drinking and bathing places, you can reasonably sit back and relax. Your birds are well cared for. But if you are prepared to go one step further, you can give yourself a great deal of extra pleasure. By providing food, you can entice the birds to show themselves more freely in places where you can watch them. And as the availability of food controls to some extent the bird population in your garden, you will also be increasing their numbers. But providing food is not a pleasure to be undertaken lightly. Put out some scraps and you will soon attract new residents. They will become dependent on your generosity, and if it fails, they will be competing for a previously—and still—inadequate supply of natural foods. In cold or wet weather especially, birds may lose a lot of weight overnight, and they have to make it up again during the brief hours of daylight. Death comes in a matter of hours even to a healthy small bird, if it is without food in very cold weather. In winter the real killer is hunger, not cold.

The problems are simple enough to list: what to provide, and how to serve it? You may think it sufficient simply to toss bread scraps on the lawn, but this will not do at all. Bread, especially mass-produced white bread, is about as good for birds as it is for us, and certainly does not constitute a satisfactory diet. Besides, some birds do not care to come down to ground level for their food, some birds do not eat bread at all, and in any case, there is always the threat of a cat waiting in the wings! Some birds are carnivorous and others vegetarian. It is no good to offer a worm to a White-throated Sparrow, or a sunflower seed to a Phoebe. A quick glance at a bird's bill will give a clue to its diet. Finches have a nutcracker or seedcracker bill, adapted to split and crack, and they feed mostly on grain and seeds. They are hard-billed birds. Woodpeckers have exceedingly hard bills although their food is soft; the bill is used as a chisel, probe and pick. Birds with soft bills such as thrushes, warblers, and flycatchers are limited in their diet to grubs, caterpillars and other soft food. The hard-billed birds, however, will feed on some insect and animal life in warm weather (and collect it for their young), and some soft-billed birds will take small seeds in winter, when hungry. At our bird table we must provide both.

NATURAL FOOD. The best food to provide is what the birds would

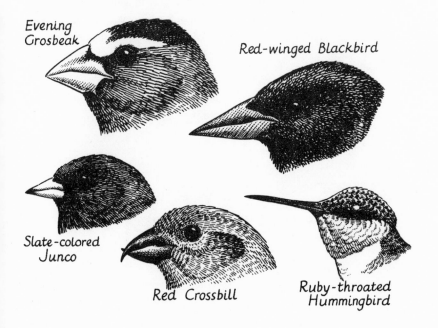

Evening Grosbeak

Red-winged Blackbird

Slate-colored Junco

Red Crossbill

Ruby-throated Hummingbird

choose for themselves unaided. One way to do this is to go on a nut and berry collecting expedition in the autumn. From August to October, you will be able to collect a fine harvest from the edges of rural highways and fields. Pick the berries when they are just ripe.

Among the berries that may be harvested in the wild are catbrier, wild raspberry, bayberry (wax myrtle), pokeberry, highbush blueberry, elderberry, wild cherry, honeysuckle, fox grape, among dozens of others. Crab apples are worth collecting, and in bad weather you will find several species coming to the bird table for them. As for nuts, butternut or hazel is the best; acorns attract jays.

Dry the berries, and store both berries and nuts in a dry, dark place; they will keep until you need them. Gather pine cones and pry the seeds from between the woody scales—or keep them intact for hanging. Store all seeds, including weed-seeds such as thistle, wild grasses (*Panicum sp.*), ragweed, dandelion, etc., in muslin bags, hung up where the air can get at them.

KITCHEN SCRAPS. Many people will tell you that birds love bread, and though this is true, nobody would suggest that birds can live on bread alone. It is better than nothing, and whole wheat is better than white. Stale cake is good, especially if homemade with a high protein content. Minced raw meat, meat bones, cooked and chopped bacon rinds and cheese are all good. Doughnuts are a favored food by some species, as are potato chips. The best kitchen scrap offering of all is suet, which can be offered uncooked and separately, or used as a binding material for bird pudding

or seed cakes. Almost everything except highly seasoned or salty food can go into the basket for bird scraps. Don't worry about giving birds something that won't agree with them; they will select what suits them and leave the rest. One way or another, you will find that not much is wasted.

COMMERCIAL BIRD FOOD. In these days when wild bird food is provided in the supermarket along with the corn flakes and the frozen lobster tails, it hardly seems necessary to dwell at length on this subject. At present writing a fairly acceptable (readily gobbled up) mixture is available at local markets for about $1.99 per 25-pound bag, or about 8¢ per pound. According to the printed analysis on the bag, it includes sunflower seeds, milo, wheat, red, yellow and white millet and hulled oats. A slightly more expensive mixture, lists the same ingredients, with peanut hearts added. Peanut hearts, chopped up, is one of the richest (in oil) and most useful of bird seed foods. It can be bought separately and used to enrich other mixtures.

Such commonly obtained mixtures are suitable for most seedeating birds, although such ground feeders as pheasant, Bobwhite and Mourning Dove will be more attracted to cracked or whole corn, such as that obtained from feed stores under the name of "chick cracked corn" in 25, 50 or 100-pound bags.

Sunflower seeds are beloved of Blue Jays, chickadees, Evening Grosbeaks and many others, and happily the small-sized seeds are both a better bargain and better for the birds.

Other seeds that are often found in wild bird mixtures that are sold commerically are rape and hemp, the latter being one of the finest of all seed foods.

If you prefer to mix your own recipe, you will probably find that you will be able to provide a more nutritious bird table at lower cost. Listed in Appendix B are several seed wholesalers who will ship to you, usually in no less than 100-pound bags, either the separate ingredients or a mixture to your own specifications. While 100 pounds may seem to be a sizable order of wild bird seed food, an active bird table may well consume several pounds a day, and your savings will be considerable over the winter.

Other seed foods that have been recommended are pumpkin and watermelon seeds (run them through a coarse food mill before serving), rice, chopped oats and whole wheat. Peanuts in the shell are excellent bird food, and strung together as in the picture they are playthings for chickadees, nuthatches and Blue Jays.

Peanut butter is equally nutritious, but *do not feed it straight.* It can, when fed as it comes from the jar, actually kill small birds by caking in their mandibles and preventing the birds from feeding entirely. It should always be mixed well with equal parts of corn meal. In this form it can be poked into specially prepared "peanut butter logs," holes in tree trunks, smeared on rough bark or served in one of the many available feeders designed for this purpose.

Here are some seed mixtures recommended by various authorities:

National Audubon Society
Bread, dried and ground, 5 parts
Meat, ground and dried, 3 parts
Millet, 3 parts
Ant eggs, 2 parts
Sunflower seed, 3 parts
Dried berries (raisins, currants) 1½ parts, by weight

This is a rather expensive, high protein, balanced diet.

Thomas P. McElroy, Jr.
Sunflower 25%
Hemp 25%
Small yellow millet 20%
Large yellow or white millet 20%
Buckwheat 5%
Chick cracked corn 5%

Screech Owl

Brown Creeper

Chickadee

Downy Woodpecker

Barn Swallow

Yellow-bellied Sapsucker

Chimney Swift

White-breasted Nuthatch

Sparrow Hawk

luebird

Least Flycatcher

ellowthroat

House Wren

Cedar Waxwing

Green Heron

Mourning Dove

Kinglet

Robin

fous-sided Towhee

Purple Grackle

Chipping Sparrow

Al Martin
Small yellow millet, 2 parts
Large white millet, 2 parts
Canary seed, 1 part
Rape, 1 part
Hemp, 1 part
Niger, 1 part
Flax, 1 part
Sunflower, 1 part

Martin also adds such exotic and expensive seeds to commercial mixtures as Psyllium, "Teazle," "Gold of Pleasure," "Grains of Paradise" and Saffron, which are seed names known to, and bought by, caged-bird breeders.

Margaret McKenny
Recommends a seed cake made by melting suet and adding canary seed, chopped peanuts and raisins, oatmeal, sunflower seeds, cooked and uncooked rice, scratch food (chick cracked corn), honey and sugar. A very balanced concoction.

See also Appendix A.

Other nuts besides peanuts are all worth buying, but they must be considered among the more costly luxuries of the bird table. Coconut is good, but serve it in shell, not dessicated or ground, as this will swell up inside a bird's stomach with dire results. Saw the nut in half or crack it open and hang it so that rain cannot get in.

In addition to the seed mixtures, coarse oatmeal, costing about 20¢ a pound at the food stores, can be offered raw, but untreated raw oats are favored by many more birds. You may be able to arrange with your local fruit store or the produce manager of your supermarket for a box of unsaleable fruit to be kept aside for you. Apples, oranges, tomatoes, grapefruit, bananas and grapes are all equally acceptable if you cut them up. Orioles are particularly fond of oranges. In hard times, birds will eat the fruit ravenously, but in cold weather suet should be added, because it provides energy so efficiently.

For live insect food the best buys are mealworms and ant eggs. You can buy them direct from pet shops or breed them yourself.

See Appendices A and B. Serve the mealworms in a fairly deep round dish, so that they cannot escape—they are amazingly mobile.

Birds not only have varying food requirements, both in nature and at the food table, but they also have varying methods of foraging and hunting for food. Some skulk about on the ground, some snoop along the branches and some creep about on tree trunks. So we must have variety of presentation as well as variety of food.

BIRD TABLES. The traditional way of feeding is with a bird tray, although it has its limitations. The tray can be supported from a post, or it can hang from the bough of a tree or a bracket. It can be a shelf attached to a window, or most simple of all, be a bare place or a flat rock on the ground, provided it does not afford an ambush station for a cat, fox or other predator.

Each method has some advantages. The feeding tray should not be too small. Somewhere around three or four square feet is ideal, although most commercially sold feeding trays are much smaller. It should have a coaming around the edge to keep the food from being blown off, with a gap somewhere to allow for cleaning and for water runoff. Better still, it should be roofed to prevent seed being watersoaked by rain and snow, and to allow feeding after a snowfall. A feeding tray sheltered on three sides, set on a revolving pedestal or with a ball-bearing swivel, and fitted with vanes, will revolve so that it will always face away from the wind. If you are in any area where the Common Pigeon will invade your feeding trays, a screen with a $1\frac{1}{2}$-inch mesh will allow only the more desirable birds access to the food. Some commercial feeders feature a weighted landing perch that will support only the smaller, lighter species, unceremoniously dumping off the larger birds, such as pigeons. Glass on three sides is better than wood, because it allows more light on the scene, which is important if you are interested in photography.

Whether you hang it from a tree branch or a wire stretched between two trees, or between house and pole, or whether it stands on a pole alone, the tray should be about five to six feet above the ground. The safest post is an iron pipe, but any smooth pole will do. The worst support is one of those rustic affairs that positively invite squirrels and cats to climb up to their felonious work. The table should be in a position where it gets neither too much sun nor too much cold wind—the revolving weathervane approach

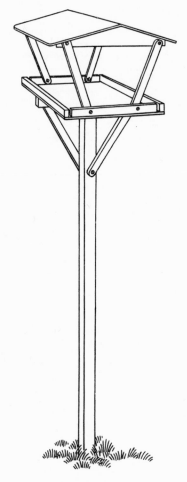

will take care of that. It should be within reasonable distance of cover—perhaps six to twelve feet—but out of cat-jumping range. For most wooden poles, a cat-squirrel guard is required, a metal sleeve or cone below the table at least 18 inches in diameter and curved downward. See page 31.

If the tray has a feed hopper, it should be kept full of mixed seed for the finches. On the tray you can distribute your offering of scraps, fruit, bird pudding and other treats. Ideally, the food should be placed in pieces either so big that birds cannot carry them away, or so small that they do not want to carry them. Medium-sized pieces get carried to nearby bushes and get lost,

attracting mice and such. Another solution to this problem is a removable, close-mesh wire netting which fits inside the coaming, covers the food and prevents big birds from flying off with large lumps.

Certain birds prefer to feed on the ground, and for that purpose an open flat space, well away from possible ambush, is desirable. In our garden we use a flat composition stone about four feet in diameter on which seed and other food is spread. It is exactly 28 feet from a window, which happens to be the best focal length of our telephoto camera lens. Distance from feeding trays to camera and light source should be considerations for anyone interested in photography. Nearby is an apple tree with a suet cage, a covered feeding tray on a stand, and a second, smaller seed dispenser on a pole. The apple tree serves as a *queue* for birds waiting their turn. All are within camera range.

Scrap Baskets. The advantage of scrap baskets is that the food is less likely to be blown about and scattered. The disadvantage is that some birds cannot manage to hang on to them when they are suspended. A serviceable scrap basket is one of those netting bags that are used to hold potatoes, onions or oranges at the supermarket. However, it will soon get messy, and it is best to buy a basket specially made for the job. Many garden supply stores sell special mesh bags for this purpose, or for suet, for about 60¢.

Scrap baskets made of collapsible wire mesh must be avoided, since a bird may get a foot jammed between two moving pieces of wire. Sharp edges and potential leg-damagers must in fact be watched for on all feeding devices. Many small birds get leg injuries, and we are not sure that bird feeders are not often to blame.

Seed Hoppers. The only practical way of providing seed is from a hopper. All other ways are very wasteful. It is important to keep the seed dry, and a hopper does this admirably. You can fit one into your revolving bird table or window ledge tray (see the illustration on page 34), but there are many simple and inexpensive seed hoppers on the market. A perfectly adequate one can be made with the glass from a hurricane lamp suspended ½-inch above the tray by means of nails, and roofed over with a hinged roof to allow refilling. Keep the hopper well filled with mixed seeds, and do not risk a supply failure in bad weather, because the birds will have become dependent on your generosity.

Nuts. Peanuts are a bird's best friend, and a good way to present them is to have a special wire-netting box, preferably with a solid roof to keep the shelled nuts dry. You may find yourself buying two pounds of nuts a week, but it will be in a good cause. If you hang whole peanuts, the best plan is to take a thin length of galvanized wire about 18 inches long and cut it obliquely at one end to make a sharp point on which to skewer the nuts. Bend the top end into a hanging hook and the bottom end up slightly to prevent the peanuts from sliding off. Attach the wire to its anchor point by a rubber band, and the whole thing will twist around as the birds perch on it. The peanut skewer can hang from the bird table or from another place inaccessible to squirrels.

Suet Cakes. Cakes of suet in various shapes to fit commercially sold holders are available everywhere, but it is easy and less expensive to make your own. Merely take a bell-mouthed or cup-shaped container, fill it with a mixture of scraps, seeds and melted suet (or the McKenny-style mixture, page 40) and let it cool. If a loop of cord is inserted in the middle while the mixture is being poured, it will serve as a convenient hanger when the suet cake is removed from the mold with a knife. If wooden or wire holders are available, of course, no hanger is needed.

Another useful hanging device is a suet or peanut butter log, available in supply shops or easily made. A short length of birch log is bored with one-inch holes; the holes are stuffed with suet or peanut butter-cornmeal mixture and hung up. Woodpeckers are very fond of this gadget, but avoid any fancy perches or the Starlings will soon take over. And never hang up suet where it is unprotected from rain and sun.

 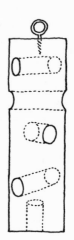

WINDOW SILLS. Even if you do not have a garden, you can still have a lot of fun providing a specialized bird feeding station at your window sill. You might devise a special adapter for clamping the bird tray to a sill, and most of the hanging seed hoppers and feeders can be suspended from a bracket. Even if you have a splendid garden, a window sill feeding tray is desirable because, since House Sparrows and Starlings are shy of it, you will be able to put out special delicacies for special birds. If possible, use a window sill that is reasonably sheltered from both hot sun and cold winds. And whatever feeding arrangements you may have, remember that a constant supply of water is absolutely essential.

SELECTION PROBLEMS. Some people have a most unreasonable hatred of Starlings, although they do perform valuable services in controling the Japanese beetle by eating the grubs as they emerge from our lawns. But Starlings—and House Sparrows too—can by their sheer numbers and bullying ways rather overwhelm one's facilities.

One way to cheat the Starlings is to feed early or late. Starlings are late risers, and as they flock away to roost early in the afternoon, you can foil them with early morning and late afternoon feeds

for your wanted visitors. Another trick is to make a feeding cage of wire mesh with an aperture too narrow for Starlings. If you put 1⅛-inch mesh around your bird table, it should keep the Starlings out. Several commercially sold feeding trays are protected by wire mesh, but one popular variety has a mesh so large that it admits Mourning Doves and squirrels, and obviously, Starlings. The only disadvantage of the smaller mesh is that it also excludes Cardinals and birds of comparable size, while admitting House Sparrows.

Starlings and House Sparrows tend to be more easily disturbed than other birds, so if you provide a feeding patch for them well away from your house and bird table, they may patronize it in preference to the home feeding trays. Then too, we have found that dried stale bread, broken up and tossed on the ground some distance from the main feeders will keep the Starlings and House Sparrows busy while the more desirable birds are enjoying your more expensive food. But almost any really busy feeder will have its share—sometimes a major share—of House Sparrows. The only known way to control them is to trap and ruthlessly eliminate them, a practice which, while it is within the law, goes against the instincts of most bird lovers. Personally, we find that although House Sparrows more than double the cost of keeping our bird table, they are brash, intelligent and amusing, their presence attracts other species, and at worst they are a mixed blessing.

WHEN TO FEED. The best method, by far, is to feed at the same time every day. Animals have built-in clocks and appreciate regularity. Early morning is the best time of all, as birds lose weight and water overnight and need a good start to the day. Clearly, the most important season is winter, when natural food supplies are lowest (late winter in particular, when the natural berry crop is gone). During a hard cold spell with snow, you will hold the lives of many small birds in your hands. In fact, it is better not to operate a feeding station at all than to attract a dependent following of birds into the winter and then abandon them, even for a few days. It is true that birds have feathers which insulate them from the cold, but a body cannot function and keep warm without fuel.

When spring comes, the pattern of feeding should be altered. The amounts of heating foods such as suet and hemp should be reduced, and less bread should be given, as this may fill nestling birds with low-value bulk. Nestlings of almost all our small songbirds and garden nesters are insect-eaters during this period. Put out some mealworms and ant pupae if you wish, although this is the season when birds are repaying you for your winter work. They will destroy hordes of insect pests far more successfully than any chemical insecticides.

You may wish to keep feeding through the spring, summer and early fall, but in smaller quantities. Water is more important than food in these seasons. But with summer-long service, your birds will stay with you, and when you start increasing supplies in late autumn, you will have a resident band of pensioners to help attract the winter visitants that will be arriving with every cold weather front.

HUMMINGBIRDS. Hummingbirds are strictly New World delights, and nothing like them occurs in Britain. In the area covered by this book only the Ruby-throated Hummingbird is common, and there are many areas well within its large range where it is not abundant. But if you have a wooded area nearby, or if your garden itself is comparable to a clearing in the woods, with sufficient bright flowers all summer (especially bright reds), you may attract a pair or more of these tiny friends. Feeding is simple

The feeding tray should not be too small - around three or four square feet is ideal. A coaming stops food blowing off.

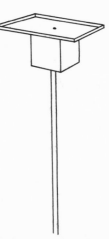

This "bird table" is made by the Royal Society for the protection of Birds in Britain where it is very popular with both birds and birders. A food hopper is shown fitted under the roof.

Gaps in the coaming make cleaning easier.

A food basket for scraps or nuts is very popular with chickadees.

A galvanised tube or smooth pole is ideal.

About five or six feet high.

A biscuit tin fixed under the table is a useful anti-squirrel device.

with one of the many varieties of inexpensive feeding devices now being advertised. Or you can fashion your own feeding tubes using chemist's test tubes (about 3-inches long), clamped or wired to hang at an angle convenient to the birds, set on stakes four or more feet high in your garden's flower beds, or hung from shrubbery or the house itself near an observation window. (See the illustration below.) Other containers, such as pill bottles, vials and individual cream servers may be used. It is said that a red bow or a red plastic flower tied to the container helps to attract the hummers to newly set-out feeders.

As for food, the usual menu is sugar water—water into which sugar has been melted—one part sugar to two parts water. Since sugar is pure carbohydrate without protein or minerals, a far more nutritious mixture is honey and water in a one-to-three mixture. The honey is dissolved in hot water and the mixture boiled briefly to prevent fermentation. Red food coloring added to the syrup will make it more attractive to the hummers. McElroy lists a special hummer diet formulated by the New York Zoological Society designed to keep its caged hummingbirds in tip-top condition. Since these birds do not have the available supply of insects with which your wild hummers will supplement their honey water diet, they are in greater need of a balanced formula than the wild birds. But you may wish to try it.

Many flowering trees and shrubs, as well as garden flowers, attract hummingbirds. Among the most favored are TRUMPET VINE, *Campsis radicans;* TRUMPET HONEYSUCKLE, *Lonicera sempervirens;* BEAUTY BUSH, *Kolkwitzia amabilis;* BUTTERFLY BUSH, *Buddleia sp.;* WEIGELA, *Weigela sp.* Also CARDINALFLOWER, *Lobelia cardinalis;* COLUMBINE, *Aquilegia, sp.;* CORAL BELLS, *Heuchera sanguinea;* BEE BALM, *Monarda sp.;* FOXGLOVE, *Digitalis sp.;* SNAPDRAGON, *Antirrhinum, sp.;* SCARLET SALVIA, *Salvia splendens;* GARDEN SAGE, *Salvia officinalis,* and many others. Among trees, PEA TREE, *Caragana arborescens,* MIMOSA TREE, *Albizzia julibrissin* and HORSE CHESTNUT, *Aesculus hippocastanum* seem especially favored.

5 Predators and Poisons

A wild bird's life is filled with natural perils. After surviving a cold winter, it may get snapped up by a Cooper's Hawk. If it succeeds in finding a mate and hatching young, there may be a sudden shortage of food and the weaker nestlings may die. The chances of a wild bird living to a ripe old age are so remote as to be almost non-existent. (Small birds like Cardinals may live to be eight or ten years old in the protected comfort of zoo cages, but average less than two years of life expectancy in the wild.) So if we are going to invite birds to join us in our gardens, we are obliged to try to reduce the hazards.

Ideally, of course, you should completely seal your garden from unwelcome predators, but this is more easily said than done. Hawks, owls, shrikes and other avian predators are all part of the natural scene, but domestic cats are most certainly not. There is no place for them in a bird garden, but you will never keep them out short of total war. If you have a cat of your own, you may consider keeping it indoors for a reasonable and regular period each morning and before dusk in order to give the birds time to feed. Or even raise your cat as would an apartment dweller whose cat never knows that there is a world outside the walls of his home. We must admit that we like cats for their animated and decorative presence *indoors,* but the fact remains that the United States and Canada harbor millions of cats, every one of these detrimental to a good bird garden. You must make your own decision, but one thing is certain. You should not try to tame your garden birds if you keep a cat. Feed them and make homes for them by all means, but don't encourage them to become too friendly or you will, inevitably, be providing food for a cat garden, not a bird garden.

If you, and your neighbors, can put up with it, a chain link fence is undoubtedly the best defense against other people's cats (and small boys). This may seem a drastic and unsightly solution to the problem, but it is surprising how, given some care in its planning and planting, a fence can be made to blend into its background. Some of the newer chain link fences offered for sale are plastic coated in dark shades of green which make them almost disappear from a distance. The older natural metal galvanized surface can be painted dark green or tar-coated to reduce its light reflection and visibility. Use heavy gauge wire, six feet high, with about 18 inches sunk underground for rodent protection. At the top of the wire there should be an angled crossarm with two or three strands of barbed wire; without this boys, cats, and other invaders can easily scale your fence. Care should be taken to see that there are no easily climbed trees that overhang your fence; they will serve as inviting nullifiers.

If you feel you cannot go so far as installing a wire fence, the best substitute is a thick and prickly hedge. Hawthorn or holly hedges will in time become fairly impenetrable, as will multiflora rose and barberry. You will have to watch, however, for secret passageways and block them with catbrier, rose or thorn cuttings. If you have plenty of room, leave your hedges unclipped, and they will bloom and fruit. If you must clip, you will have less fruit, but you will help to provide good nesting sites. Whichever you do, allow some of the plants in your hedge to mature so that they grow out of the hedge and bear fruit. Holly is particularly good, because the dead leaves cover the soil underneath with spiny points which deter cats.

Rats have to be taken seriously. They climb well, even shinnying up trees and hedges in search of eggs and young birds, and a good bird garden is also an attractive rat garden. So food should not be left on the ground at night, and windfalls too should be cleared away every evening; they can become part of the winter bird table. The best way to deal with rats is to use a safe poison, or put plenty of traps under cover in dark places. Place a five- or six-foot drainpipe (six-inch diameter) in the likely places, and put a killer food bait—Warfarin is the safest—in the middle of it. Mechanical rat traps are only moderately successful. Rats are suspicious creatures, and if you try traps, put one on each side of a bait placed in the middle of a pipe length. Cheese, apple, cake—almost anything will serve as bait. Set the traps before dusk and examine them when it is dark. Don't set them and leave them all night or you might trap a cat or some small mammal that you might like to have around.

Gray squirrels, too, are unwelcome visitors to the bird garden. They may appear charmingly acrobatic and amusing as they leap from branch to branch or munch on a sunflower seed, but they are great egg-eaters. They will even enlarge the hole of a nest box and lift out the nestlings. You should also discourage jays, cowbirds, grackles and crows, for there is no doubt that except for the cowbird, they will take many eggs and the young of small birds; the cowbird is a menace because of its parasitic egg-laying habits. Cowbird eggs in the host bird's nest often result in crowding out the legitimate offspring, so that only the cowbird young survive. House Sparrows, Starlings, and the Common Pigeon or Rock Dove are all foreign freeloaders who will monopolize both feeders and

nesting sites unless sharply controled. While we hesitate to recommend positive destruction methods, such as trapping or shooting, many a bird garden becomes so dominated by these avian interlopers that it becomes almost futile to set out food, for our native wild birds are crowded out, and the expense is all out of proportion to the good. In such a case, drastic measures are necessary. Some bird garden enthusiasts report that they can curtail visits by cats and squirrels by the judicious use of non-lethal but stinging pellets from a slingshot or even a target air rifle. Others admit frankly using a pellet gun or rifle to kill. One suburbanite of our acquaintance admits having dispatched over a hundred cats from his half-acre plot in this manner, shooting downward from an upstairs window. A risky business at best, and in many locations quite illegal.

With the smaller birds such as House Sparrow, Starling and cowbird, trapping or netting is the only effective means of control. If you cannot quite get yourself to kill small birds, no matter how obnoxious, you might try transporting them (more than twenty miles from home), although usually most of them will be back home almost as soon as you are. (Squirrels can be transported with greater success but even they have strong homing instincts.) Caution: check your local laws before instituting any program of predator control, even for unprotected species. And your conscience.

The greatest bird menace of all, today, is the residual chlorinated hydrocarbon insecticide. After years of trial and a growing weight of evidence against them, it is depressing to find that farmers, tree growers, municipalities and other government agencies and even conservation organizations still use and recommend dangerous sprays and seed-dressings, and that garden supply stores everywhere still sell harmful and extravagantly overpowerful garden "aids." If you have the least feeling for wildlife, and incidentally, if you value your own health, you should refuse to use chlorinated hydrocarbons as pesticides, especially any that contain forms of DDT or the D.E.A.T.H. group, including Dieldrin, Endrin, Aldrin, Toxaphene and Heptachlor. Our environment is becoming increasingly polluted with chemicals whose long-term effects are largely unknown but highly suspect. Most of the DDT-D.E.A.T.H. group are non-degradable, meaning that they do not break down in the soil or in animal fatty tissues, and thus linger in the food chain for months and years. Some of the poisons sprayed on farm, forest and city shade trees wash down into the ocean, and already all the waters of the earth are contaminated with them. (Petrels that feed far from land, such as the Bermuda Petrel, are showing high concentrations of DDT in their eggs and a reduced rate of breeding success, almost certainly as a result.)

Many of the pesticides sold freely in garden supply stores are dangerous, not only to the pests they set out to destroy (some of which are rapidly building up an immunity to them!), but to useful animals as well, and ultimately to ourselves. The insects killed or half-killed by such substances are eaten by birds, and the poison the insect contained is not completely excreted by the bird, but some is stored in its fat. Other birds and mammals feed on these birds and obtain much larger doses, which they in turn accumulate. These dangerous substances are likely to build up especially harmful levels in birds and mammals at the end of long food chains, the carnivorous ones. Poisoning of this kind may not only kill, but it also appears to affect fertility by inhibiting the function of the sex hormones and by weakening egg shells. The drastic decline in fertility and reproductive success of the species at the end of food chains, such as the Osprey, the Bald Eagle and the Peregrine Falcon, which has virtually disappeared as a breeding species from our entire area, has been attributed to the pesticide factor by many experts.

This is not to suggest that we stop waging war against pests, but it is worth pointing out that sprays do dangerously what birds do safely. Finches, flycatchers, warblers and thrushes all patrol and police leafy places and decimate the caterpillar and insect population. Thrushes help with your snails and slugs. Encourage the birds, save yourself money and give yourself pleasure at the same time. It is true that birds will also eat some of your soft fruit and spoil some of the buds of your fruit trees, but this is a small price to pay for the knowledge that yours is a poison-free garden. On balance, birds do more good than harm.

The Department of Agriculture and various other research organizations have recommended that gardeners not use the D.E.A.T.H. group of pesticides. Note that the brand names on the labels do not always identify (and usually do not indicate) these chemicals. One must read the small print on the label, can

or spray to discover whether the list of ingredients includes dangerous compounds.

DDT, BHC, Lindane and Chlordane are non-degradable chlorinated hydrocarbons, too. Their use should be avoided. Be careful
with half-empty and even empty containers; dispose of them in
such a way that their contents cannot contaminate soil or water.
Any chemical should be used sparingly, with care, exactly according
to the directions on the label; ideally, it should not be used at
all. Herbicides such as 2,4-D and 2,4,5-T are also dangerous.

Some insecticides appear today to be reasonably safe. Pyrethrum
and derris and rotenone, for example, are potent insect killers which
are not harmful to warm-blooded creatures. They do not accumulate, to be passed through the food chain. Nicotine and malathion
also do not accumulate, but are more poisonous and require more
caution in handling. Derris is dangerous to fish, so do not use
it if there is any likelihood of it finding its way into a pond or
stream. The pesticide compound sold as Sevin is now being tested
and is reportedly safer than other chlorinated hydrocarbons in recommended doses.

Pyrethins are extracted from a white-flowered crop grown in
the highlands of Kenya and are the basis for a number of safe
pesticides. As insects do not seem to build up resistance to pyrethrum, it is more efficient in the long run, although it may not
have the sensational and immediate effect of some of the more
dangerous hydrocarbons. But use the spray in the evening, to spare
the bees. Pyrethrum will control most flying and crawling insects.

6 Species Notes: Birds Which Use Nest Boxes or Visit Feeding Stations

There are no identification notes in the following list, but the numbers immediately following the common names of the birds refer to the page number of the species description in *A Field Guide to the Birds* by Roger Tory Peterson, which is in every birdwatcher's library. As in that volume, the birds are arranged in the order devised for the American Ornithologists' Union *Checklist of North American Birds,* Fifth Edition and A.O.U.-accepted names are used. Further information on habitat, distribution, food and behavior can be found in the various volumes cited in the Bibliography. Further information on attracting these species with food, housing and planting can be found in numerous books also listed in the Bibliography. The birds included in this section are only those that might be induced to nest in your garden through materials or sites provided by you, or attracted to your garden by food, water or plantings provided by you. Many other species of birds may casually visit your garden during migration, or nest in woodlands, marshes or fields on your property without any inducement from you. To include them all would be to provide information on most of the birds on the eastern North American list.

MUTE SWAN. 30. *Cygnus olor.* A locally common introduced resident in the northeastern U.S., found in parks and estates, where it is now mostly wild.

Dips head and neck or tips up to graze on underwater vegetation; also takes small frogs, tadpoles, fish. Will come to hand or feeding station for scraps, barley, corn, wheat.

Nests almost anywhere near water, in a large heap of vegetation. Nestbox: artificial island or raft, primed with a pile of vegetation.

3–11 eggs, almost white, tinged with grayish or bluish-green. April–June. Incubation, about 35 days; fledging, about 4½ months. One brood. Warning! Aggressive at nest or with cygnets.

Read: Kortwright, F. H., *The Ducks, Geese, and Swans of North America,* American Wildlife Institute (1943), Washington, D.C.

CANADA GOOSE. 31. *Branta canadensis.* Widely distributed migrant, wintering bird and semi-domesticated breeding species. Frequents grasslands, lakes, ponds and bays.

Grazes in flocks on grasslands, grain fields. Also takes water plants. Will come to hand feed on corn or bread when tame. Wild flocks will come in to tame decoys.

Nests on islands and marshes, sheltered by underbrush. Nest: hollow, lined with grasses, leaves, reeds, down and feathers. Artificial nest-site: a box or platform raised on posts above the water level or on a raft. Make an artificial island: plant clumps of iris, cattail, sedge, etc., to provide an artificial nest-site, with a willow for shelter. Warning: can be very aggressive (especially gander) in breeding season.

5–6 white eggs. Late March–April. Incubation, 4 weeks; fledging, 6 weeks. One brood.

Read: Kortwright, F. H., *The Ducks, Geese, and Swans of North America.* Bent, A. C., "Life Histories of North American Water Fowl, Part 2," *U.S. National Museum Bulletin 130* (1925): 204–236.

MALLARD. 36. *Anas platyrhynchos.* Common to abundant in fresh water ponds, marshes, also semi-domestic in park and estate ponds. Breeds from s. Ontario south to s. Kansas, Illinois, Ohio and n. Virginia; winters roughly from the 40th parallel southward.

Feeds by tipping up, on aquatic vegetation and on water insects, snails, fish. Will come to corn or bread or other grains scattered in shallow water or on water's edge.

Nests in thick undergrowth not far from water in marshes, estuaries, etc. Sometimes in tree holes, second-hand crow nests, etc. Nest lined with grass, leaves, reeds, feathers, down. Artificial nesting: try providing a bushel basket in a typical nest-site. Where Mallards have become very tame, try erecting an open-ended barrel on an island.

About 12 eggs, grayish-green or greenish-buff, occasionally clear blue. March, onwards. Incubation, by female 4 weeks; fledging, 7½ weeks. One or two broods.

Read: Kortwright, F. H., *The Ducks, Geese, and Swans of North America*. Bent, A. C., "Life Histories of North American Wild Fowl, Part 1," *U.S. National Museum Bulletin 126* (1923): 34–47.

Wood Duck. 43. *Aix sponsa*. Widely distributed but never abundant breeding bird almost throughout the area south of s. Canada, wintering in southern and Gulf states.

Feeds at water's edge or on land on water plants, acorns, berries, seed grains, insects, spiders, mollusks.

Nests in woodlands adjacent to or over water, occasionally in

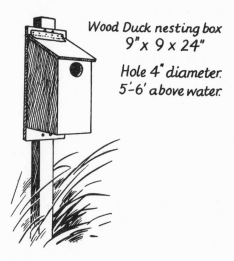

Wood Duck nesting box
9" x 9 x 24"

Hole 4" diameter.
5'-6' above water.

trees some distance from water, or in barns or outbuildings. Uses natural cavities in trees, as high as 60 feet, and will use properly constructed and placed nestboxes in marshy woodlands. See drawing on page 60 for details. Houses over water can be as low as three feet, over land at least eight feet high to avoid human molestation. The posts or trees should be protected from predators, especially raccoons, with wide sheet-metal cones or 3-foot wide sheet-metal sheathing.

10–15 dull white or creamy eggs. Nesting, April–June. Incubation, 28–32 days by female; fledging, 7–8 weeks.

Read: Kortwright, F. H., *The Ducks, Geese, and Swans of North America.* Bent, A. C., "Life Histories of North American Wild Fowl, Part 1." Webster, Clark G., "Better Nest Boxes for Wood Ducks," *U.S. Fish & Wildlife Service Leaflet 393,* Washington, D.C.

AMERICAN KESTREL (SPARROW HAWK). 74. *Falco sparverius.* Resident throughout the area, except in winter in the far north. A bird of farmlands, open country, woodland edge, often open spaces bordering densely populated areas.

Perches on trees, posts, wires or buildings; hunts in the open, often hovering above its prey: grasshoppers, mice, rarely small birds.

Makes no nest, but lays eggs in a hollow, or on a ledge of

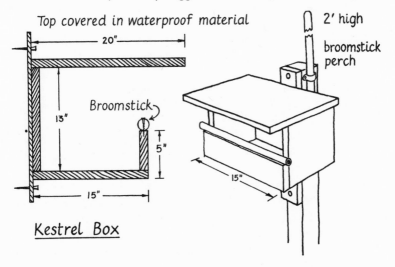

Top covered in waterproof material   2' high

broomstick perch

20"

13"

Broomstick

5"

15"

15"

Kestrel Box

a building or in a woodpecker hole or nestbox. Standard shape bird house, 8-inches square, 15-inches high with a 3-inch opening, 10-inches above the floor. Should be 18–40 feet above ground. A broomstick projecting two feet above the box will serve as a convenient perch. See illustration on page 61.

About five eggs (2–7), the white color often hidden by red-brown markings. Mid-April onwards. Incubation, 28–30 days mainly by female; fledging, 28 days. One brood.

Read: Bent, A. C., "Life Histories of North American Birds of Prey, Part 2," *U.S. National Museum Bulletin 170* (1938): 106–121. Willoughby, E. J. and Cade, T. J., "Breeding Behavior of the American Kestrel (Sparrow Hawk)," *Living Bird, 3* (1964): 75–159. (Ithaca, New York: Cornell Laboratory of Ornithology.)

BOBWHITE. 77. *Colinus virginianus.* One of America's most popular game birds, common in brushy fields, woodland edge and farmlands from Nebraska, s. Great Lakes and mid-New York southward, where it is a resident.

Feeds on seeds and fruits of hundreds of plants and takes insect food in summer. Will come to feeders from nearby fields and brushy areas or from pine woods in the south, for various seed foods, berries and water if placed on the ground. Plantings of various cereal grains should be ¼-acre per covey. An excellent food plant for Bobwhites, not favored by other birds, is *Lespedeza.*

Nests on the ground, in thickly tangled vegetation or clumps of dried grasses.

Eggs 15–20, dull white, mostly April–May (March–August). Incubation, 23–24 days by both sexes; fledging, 7 days or less, but young birds follow parent birds from nest soon after hatching. One brood is normal, occasionally two or three.

Read: Stoddard, H. L., *The Bobwhite Quail: its habits, preservation, and increase* New York: Scribner, (1931). Bent, A. C., "Life Histories of North American Gallinaceous Birds," *U.S. National Museum Bulletin 162* (1932): 9–36. Stanger, M. A., *That Quail, Robert* (Philadelphia: Lippincott), 1966.

RING-NECKED PHEASANT. 77. *Phasianus colchicus.* Introduced, now common resident game bird in farming country, more open suburbs, marsh and woodland edge. From s. Saskatchewan and s. Ontario south to n. Oklahoma, s. Indiana, Maryland.

Forages on the ground for a variety of plant and animal food:

grains, seeds, berries, insects, worms, snails. Will come to the secluded garden ground feeder for grain.

Nests in dense cover in fields, along fences, in thickets, making a hollow on the ground and lining it with grass. Encouraged to nest by undisturbed fencerows, roadsides, by planting of multiflora hedges, by late mowing of fields and by leaving a narrow border of standing grain in fields.

8–18 olive-brown eggs. Early April onwards. Incubation, 22–27 days; fledging, 12–14 days. One brood.

Read: Bent, A. C., "Life Histories of North American Gallinaceous Birds," *Bulletin 162:* 310–322. McAtee, W. L., *The Ring-necked Pheasant and its management in North America,* American Wildlife Institute (1945). Allen, D. L., *Pheasants in North America,* American Wildlife Institute (1956).

Rock Dove. 127. *Columba livia.* The common "pigeon" introduced and resident throughout temperate North America in cities, towns and around farms.

Feeds on the ground in fields, garbage dumps, on beaches and where fed in city parks. Often comes to the bird table, where it can be a ravenous nuisance. Takes most small grains, peanuts, kitchen scraps.

Nests on building ledges, under bridges, occasionally on a cliff or quarry ledge. Nests almost year round, with two or three broods annually. The nest is a messy heap of debris.

Two white eggs. Incubation, 17–19 days; fledging, 4–5 weeks.

Mourning Dove. 127. *Zenaidura macroura.* Common resident and migrant throughout the book area except in Canada and n. New England, where it summers only. Almost ubiquitous, preferring weedy fields, parks, woodland edges and gardens.

The handsome Mourning Dove will come to garden feeding tables and to water for bathing and drinking; numbers of them now apparently survive northern winters every year, thanks to man's generosity. Over 100 known foods—all vegetable—including grains, grass and weed seeds, berries and fruit.

The nest is an openwork platform of twigs and fibers in a tree, often a conifer, but it will nest on the ground in treeless country.

Two eggs, white. Incubation, 14–16 days; fledging, 10–12 days. 2–5 broods annually, from February–November.

Read: Bent, A. C., *Bulletin 162:* 402–416. Hanson, S. C., and

Kossack, C. W., *The Mourning Dove in Illinois*. (Free from Illinois Natural History Survey, Urbana, Illinois.)

GROUND DOVE. 127. *Columbigallina passerina*. Common resident bird on the coastal plain of the far south from South Carolina to Texas, in dry, weedy fields, piney woodlands, along dirt roads, in gardens.

Feeds entirely on grains and seeds such as corn, rice, chickweed, panicum, sorghum. Attracted to garden feeders by small grains and seeds scattered on the ground.

Uses a wide range of nest-sites, from the ground to a low tree crotch, often in low vegetation, vines, etc. The nest is a delicate platform of fibers. Very tame around the nest.

Two white eggs. Breeding season long: February–late October. Incubation, 12–14 days; fledging, 11 days. Two or more broods.

Read: Bent, A. C., "Life Histories of North American Gallinaceous Birds," *U.S. National Museum Bulletin 162* (1932): 435–440.

BARN OWL. 132. *Tyto alba*. Resident and non-migrant in towns and rural areas, even cities, from Gulf states north to s. Wisconsin, s. Ontario and New England. Haunts belfreys, barns, abandoned water towers with open windows, nest holes in trees.

Feeds chiefly on rodents; also takes birds. Abroad at dusk, when its hunting day begins.

A standard nestbox, 10 × 18 inches in floor area, 15–18 inches deep, with a 6-inch entrance hole 4 inches above the floor may attract Barn Owls if set high inside a barn, tower or steeple.

Eggs white, 5–8, from December (Florida) to June, mostly March to mid-April. Incubation, 26–34 days by female; fledging, 9–12 weeks. One brood, rarely two.

Read: Bent, A. C., *U.S. National Museum Bulletin 170 Part 2* (1938): 140–153.

SCREECH OWL. 132. *Otus asio*. Perhaps our commonest owl, resident in rural and suburban areas from the U.S.-Canadian border and s. Ontario south.

Feeds on small rodents, crayfish, insects and birds.

Nests in woodpecker holes and will occupy nestboxes of the standard shape, with an 8-inch square floor, 12–15 inches deep, with a 3-inch diameter entrance, 9–12 inches above the floor. Line the bottom with sawdust. Place against a tree trunk 10–30 feet high.

White eggs, 3–8 (normally 4–5) are laid, from April–July. Incubation is about 26 days; fledging 5–6 weeks. Two broods.

If you are fascinated by owls, you may think it worthwhile to have a nesting pair of these "feathered tigers," but they will decimate your small bird population in return for your hospitality.

SAW-WHET OWL. 137. *Aegolius acadicus.* The smallest, tamest owl in our area. Breeds from the mountains of West Virginia and Oklahoma north almost to the tree line in Canada.

Feeds chiefly on small rodents and insects.

Nests in old woodpecker holes 14–65 feet high. A standard nest-box with a 6-inch square floor, 12 inches deep, with a 2½-inch entrance hole about 9 inches above the floor, may be occupied. Place it about 18 feet high against a tree trunk.

4–7 white eggs are laid, mostly in April or May. Incubation, 26 days; fledging, 27–34 days. One brood.

The occasional small bird taken by this charming little owl is small penalty to pay for his presence.

Read: Bent, A. C., *Bulletin 170 Part 2:* 228–243.

RUBY-THROATED HUMMINGBIRD. 140. *Archilochus colubris.* Our tiniest species is a fairly common summer resident throughout the book area, north to s. Canada.

The hummingbird feeds on the wing, hovering before tubular flowers from which it can sip nectar; it also takes insects with its long, curved bill. Hummingbirds feed on a host of flowering trees, shrubs and garden flowers, preferring red, but brightness is more important than shade. They will come to special hummingbird feeders (see page 50).

Nests in trees around gardens or in woodland glades; its favorite nesting trees include apple, beech, birch, hemlock, maple, oak, pear and sweetgum. Nest from 6–50 feet high near or over water, usually the tiny cup is on the saddle of a down-sloping branch.

Two eggs, white. May–June. Incubation, 11–14 days by female; fledging, 14–28 days. 2–3 broods.

Read: Mason, C. R., "Invite Hummingbirds into your Garden," *Bulletin of the Massachusetts Audubon Society, Vol. 39* (1955): 217–221. Greenewalt, C. H., *Hummingbirds,* New York: Doubleday & Co. (1960).

RUFOUS HUMMINGBIRD. 141. *Selasphorus rufus.* An occasional winter visitant to the Gulf Coast from Texas to Florida. Its feeding habits are essentially the same as, but perhaps it is slightly more partial to insects than the Ruby-throated. It will come to nectar feeders.

Yellow-shafted Flicker. 141. *Colaptes auratus.* Abundant migrant and summer resident throughout the area, present in winter in reduced numbers north to the U.S.-Canadian border.

Frequent gardens, woods, orchards and parks, wherever there are sizable trees.

Omnivorous, probing for insect food "woodpecker style" on trees and telephone poles, but also showing a fondness in season for fruits and berries of many kinds, and in winter for suet and peanut butter mix at feeders. Often feeds on the ground.

Flickers will nest in bird boxes (see illustration on page 26) of the standard type, lined with wood shavings.

Eggs, 4–8, pure white, March to June. Incubation, 11–12 days by the female by day, the male at night; fledging, 25–28 days. A single brood.

At the western edge of the book area, the RED-SHAFTED FLICKER, *Colaptes cafer,* replaces this species. It has similar habits.

Read: Bent, A. C., "Life Histories of North American Woodpeckers," *U.S. National Museum Bulletin 174* (1939): 259–299. Burns, F. L., "Monograph of the Flicker," *Wilson Bulletin 7* (1900): 1–82.

Pileated Woodpecker. 142. *Dryocopus pileatus.* Uncommon but widespread forest resident throughout the book area north to s. Canada.

Handsome, crow-sized and shy, Pileateds occasionally venture in winter to feeders near wooded areas, and even (very rarely) nest in bird boxes.

Their food is typical for woodpeckers: ants and beetles, as well as the fruits and seeds of many trees and shrubs. May be attracted by suet, hamburger meat, pork rind, nutmeats.

According to Davison, has been known to nest in bird boxes with a 3–4 inch entrance cut 10–12 inches above an 8-inch square floor, and placed 12 or more feet high in a large tree in the woods. The average for natural nest-sites is 45 feet high, and the entrance is usually on the east or south side.

Eggs, 3–5, white, from late March (Florida) to June. Incubation,

18 days or more by both sexes; fledging, 26 days. There is one brood.

Read: Bent, A. C., *Bulletin 174:* 164–194.

RED-BELLIED WOODPECKER. 142. *Centurus carolinus.* Common and noisy resident in woodlands, orchards and rural areas in most of the book area, but is a rare visitant only in the northern border states, New England and s. Canada.

It has typical woodpecker feeding habits, searching for ants, insects, grubs, beetles in tree bark, but in colder months feeding largely on berries, fruits, nuts and grains in great variety. Will come to the bird table for suet, bread, corn, nuts, peanut butter mix.

Occasionally nests in bird boxes, standard shape, placed 12 feet high or higher against a tree trunk in the woods. It should be 6-inches square in floor dimensions, 12–14 inches deep, with a 2½-inch entrance hole at about the top of one side.

4–5 white eggs (3–8) from April–July. Incubation, 14 days; fledging, 26 days. 2–3 broods in the South. One in the North.

Read: Bent, A. C., *Bulletin 174:* 237–245.

RED-HEADED WOODPECKER. 143. *Melanerpes erythrocephalus.* Resident in roughly the same area as the preceding species, but much less common in most of its range. Prefers deciduous open woods, parks, rural areas with groves of trees.

Typical woodpecker fare: invertebrates in warm weather, fruits, nuts, berries in winter. At the bird table it selects the same foods as the Red-bellied Woodpecker, placed on the ground in a tree feeder.

Will nest in boxes using the same dimensions as for the preceding species, placed on poles or in trees about 12–15 feet from the ground.

Lays 4 to 6 white eggs, April–July. Incubation, about 14 days; fledging, about 27 days. Two broods.

Read: Bent, A. C., *Bulletin 174:* 195–211.

YELLOW-BELLIED SAPSUCKER. 143. *Sphyrapicus varius.* Breeds from New England, Ohio, Missouri (farther south in Appalachians) north to s. Canada. Winters from Gulf coast north roughly to 42nd parallel. A bird of orchard, woodlands, often parks.

Drills rows of holes in trees for sap and insects; partial to apples. Takes many insects from the bark in warm seasons. In winter feeds on berries, fruits, nuts. Will come to the feeder for fruit, berries, peanuts, suet.

Nests in holes excavated in trees, especially large dead birches.

4–7 white eggs, mid-May to mid-June. Incubation, about 14 days; fledging, about three weeks. One brood.

Read: Kilham, L., "Breeding Behavior of the Yellow-bellied Sapsucker," *Auk 79* (1962): 31–43. Bent, A. C., *Bulletin 174:* 126–141.

HAIRY WOODPECKER. 143. *Dendrocopos villosus.* Fairly common resident in deciduous woodlands throughout the book area, wandering in winter, sometimes into towns, orchards and gardens.

Feeding and nesting habits are typical of woodpeckers, coming occasionally to the bird table at the woodland edge for nutmeats, suet, peanut butter mix.

Nests in dead or livewood tree trunks in deep woods, but has been known to use nestboxes attached to woodland trees. The Hairy Woodpecker requires an entrance hole 1½-inches in diameter, 10–16 inches above a 6-inch diameter floor, with a few wood shavings at the bottom. Nest should be attached to a tree trunk 12–20 feet above the ground.

Four (3–6) white eggs, early April–mid-June. Incubation, 14 days; fledging, 21 days. One brood, but they will replace a lost clutch.

Read: Kilham, L., "Courtship and Territorial Behavior of Hairy Woodpeckers," *Auk 77* (1960): 259–269. Bent, A. C., *Bulletin 174:* 13–29.

DOWNY WOODPECKER. 144. *Dendrocopos pubescens.* Our commonest woodpecker, found throughout the book area in almost any wooded or landscaped habitat, particularly near flowing water. Resident, partially migratory.

Its food and nesting habits are similar to the larger Hairy Woodpecker, but it is more sociable and more frequently visits the feeding station, where it concentrates on suet.

Downy Woodpeckers will nest in a bark-covered bird house placed against a tree trunk 6–30 feet above ground. The entrance should be 1¼-inches in diameter, 8–12 inches above the 4-inch square floor. Put a bed of wood chips or sawdust in the bottom.

4–5 white eggs, early April–mid June. Incubation, 12 days by both sexes; fledging, 21 days. Single brood, but sometimes said to have two broods in the South.

Read: Bent, A. C., *Bulletin 174:* 45–72.

GREAT CRESTED FLYCATCHER. 147. *Myiarchus crinitus.* A common breeding bird in open deciduous woodlands from the Gulf of Mexico north to the southern provinces, west to the prairies. Migratory, wintering from s. Florida through Central America.

Feeds on a variety of insect life: beetles, crickets, moths, caterpillars and spiders, as well as berries, favoring Virginia creeper, mulberry and sassafras.

Prefers a natural cavity or old woodpecker nest in a tree, but will nest in gourds or bird houses (and a wide variety of other containers) hung 8–20 feet up in a woodland tree. The entrance diameter should be 2 inches, set 6–8 inches above a floor six inches in diameter.

Crested Flycatchers lay 6–8 creamy white eggs, spotted and lined with brown, mid-March to late July. Incubation, 13–15 days; fledging, 15–18 days. One or two broods annually.

Read: Mousley, W. H., "A study of the home life of the Northern Crested Flycatcher," *Auk 51* (1934) : 207–216.

EASTERN PHOEBE. 147. *Sayornis phoebe.* A common breeding bird of farmland and woodland, breeding from s. Canada south to Virginia, Georgia, and Mississippi (in mountains) and n. Texas. Rare west of 100th meridian. Winters from southern edge of breeding range southward.

The phoebe's food is typical for flycatchers: mostly insects in wide variety, but it will also eat berries, especially poison ivy, pokeberry, sumac, elderberry and bayberry (wax myrtle).

Phoebes nest on ledges under bridges, against the roots of fallen trees, under the eaves of buildings, usually near water. They will nest on a shelf provided them under eaves, or on a nesting platform 7-inches square with a slanting roof eight inches above it, placed 8–12 feet above the ground. (See illustration on page 23). The wood should be treated with a preservative but left unpainted.

3–5 white eggs are laid, early April to late June. Incubation, 16 days; fledging, 16–19 days. Two broods, rarely three.

Read: Bent, A. C., "Life Histories of North American Flycatchers, Larks, Swallows and their allies," *U.S. National Museum Bulletin 179* (1942) : 140–154.

TREE SWALLOW. 156. *Iridoprocne bicolor.* Common summer resident, nesting in flooded woodlands, marshes or fields near water from Virginia, Missouri and Kansas north to n. Canada. Abundant along Atlantic coast in migration. Winters along Gulf coast, in Florida, and northward along the coast to Virginia, rarely northward.

Feeds mostly on flying insects, except in fall and winter, when weed seeds and berries such as bayberry, elaeagnus and red cedar are taken.

Will nest in bird boxes set near or over water on poles 3–6 feet above ground or water level. House should be 5-inches square, with a hole 1½-inches in diameter, three inches above the floor. The Tree Swallow will also nest on gourds, mailboxes, drainpipes and its original home tree holes.

Lays 4–6 white eggs, mid-May to late June. Incubation, 13–16 days; fledging, 16–24 days. One brood. Males sometimes polygamous.

Read: Kuerzi, R. G., "Life History Studies of the Tree Swallow," *Proc. Linnaean Society of N.Y. No. 52–53* (1942) : 1–52.

BARN SWALLOW. 157. *Hirundo rustica.* Common spring and fall migrant and breeding bird throughout our area north to Newfoundland, s. Quebec to s. Saskatchewan, but breeds only locally in Gulf states. Found in rural areas, around barns and farmhouses, boathouses and summer cottages near water. Winters from Mexico to Brazil.

Like other swallows feeds on insects taken mostly on the wing, over fields, meadows and water.

It will nest under the eaves of buildings, as well as on rafters inside barns, open garages, and in accessible attics. Sometimes the Barn Swallow will build its mud-and-straw nest on a platform such as provided for the Eastern Phoebe.

The usual nest has 4–5 eggs, white with red-brown markings, mid-May to late July. Incubation, 15 days; fledging, 18–23 days. Often there are two broods.

Read: Bent, A. C., *Bulletin 179:* 439–463.

CLIFF SWALLOW. 157. *Petrochelidon pyrrhonota.* The breeding range and habitat (in our area) are almost identical to that of the Barn Swallow, but the Cliff is only locally common. Suffers from House Sparrow competition. Winters in s. South America.

Cliffs Swallows are colonial, building jug-shaped nests out of mud and straw, in groups up to hundreds which are affixed to the sides of barns, outbuildings or cliffs. Where present they may be encouraged to nest by providing a mud hole and a supply of straw, and by attaching a horizontal board along a wall under the eaves of the building. Unpainted surfaces preferred.

4–5 creamy white or pure white eggs spotted with brown, mid-April (Texas) to mid-July, mostly late May–June. Incubation, 12–14 days; fledging, 23–26 days. Two broods.

Read: Emlen, J. T., Jr., "Social Behavior in Nesting Cliff Swallows," *Condor 54* (1952): 177–199.

PURPLE MARTIN. 158. *Progne subis.* Martins are among our most popular birds, beloved for their graceful flight, their melodious twittering, and their insectivorous habits. They breed locally throughout the book area north to mid-Canada, and winter in Brazil. The distribution is spotty with wide gaps, but they prefer towns, suburbs and rural areas.

Martins are famous for occupying apartment houses, and they will move into boxes (or gourds) provided for them, from one room up to 200. A number of acceptable martin houses are advertised in bird journals and are also available at garden supply stores. Or you can make your own. (See the illustration on page 29.)

The house should be painted white and placed 15–20 feet high atop a pole in the open; proximity to water is an inducement. Remove each autumn to discourage House Sparrows, replace in early spring. So many martin houses harbor a single pair of House Sparrows that it is often said that they are the landlords, but this is unproved.

Eggs, 4–5 pure white, laid late March (Florida) to mid-July. Incubation, 12–16 days; fledging, 28–36 days. Two broods.

Read: Allen, R. W. and Nice, M. M., "A study of the breeding biology of the Purple Martin." *American Midland Naturalist 47* (1952): 606–665. Wade, J. L., "What you should know about the Purple Martin," (1967) Griggsville, Illinois.

GRAY JAY. 158. *Perisoreus canadensis.* Common resident of coniferous forests in Canada and n. New England, New York, Michigan and Minnesota.

Omnivorous. Notorious camp robber, the "Whisky Jack" or Canada Jay is known for its tameness and audacity, stealing anything edible (or even inedible) at the camp table, even prying open containers. Will come to the forest bird table for all kinds of food scraps; said to be fond of baked beans.

Nest, a bulky woven mass near the trunk of a conifer, 4–30 (usually under 12) feet high. Four grayish eggs, speckled with olive buff. Incubation, 16–18 days; fledging, 15 days. One brood.

Read: Bent, A. C., *Bulletin 191:* 1–32.

BLUE JAY. 158. *Cyanocitta cristata.* Abundant and widespread resident in woodlands, suburban areas and city parks throughout our area, north to s. Canada. Partially migratory, especially in the north.

Almost omnivorous, eating everything from fruits and berries to seeds and acorns, insects, frogs, mice, snails, and the eggs and young of other birds. Will come to the feeder for almost anything provided, including suet, peanuts, bread and the larger seeds.

The nest is a woven cup in a tree crotch, 10–15 feet high.

There are 4–6 olive or buff eggs, spotted with brown, laid mid-

March (Florida) to late August, mostly mid-April–late June. Incubation, 17–18 days; fledging, 17–21 days. One brood.

Read: Bent, A. C., "Life Histories of North American Jays, Crows, and Titmice," *U.S. National Museum Bulletin 191* (1946): 32–56.

SCRUB JAY. 159. *Aphelocoma coerulescens.* In the book area resident and locally common in pine oak—palmetto scrub in n. and central Florida.

Virtually omnivorous, preferring animal food but coming to the bird table for peanuts, suet, cracked corn, bread and sunflower seeds.

Nests in small colonies, 4–12 feet up in trees.

Eggs, 3–5, are pale green, blotched with reddish brown. Incubation, 15–17 days by both sexes; fledging, 18 days. One brood.

Read: Amadon, D., *A preliminary life history study of the Florida Jay, American Museum Novitates,* No. 1252 (1944).

BLACK-CAPPED CHICKADEE. 161. *Parus atricapillus.* This inquisitive and friendly bird is abundant in the northern half of the U.S. and s. Canada lowlands. It is replaced in the northern forests by the BOREAL CHICKADEE, 161, *Parus hudsonicus,* which wanders into n. U.S. in winter, and in the South by the CAROLINA CHICKADEE, 161, *Parus carolinensis.* The feeding and nesting habits of all three species are similar.

Chickadees feed mostly on small arthropods in summer, switching to plant food in colder months. They will come to the bird table for a variety of foods such as suet, peanut butter mix, sunflower and pumpkin seeds and some small berries.

Nesting is in tree holes which they excavate, or in a bark-covered nestbox 5–15 feet above the ground set on a tree trunk in or near woods or in a shady garden. Birches seem preferred. Add a couple of inches of sawdust or wood shavings to the bottom.

Chickadees lay 6–8 eggs (4–5 in Florida) which are white spotted with brown, mid-April to July (earlier in the South). Incubation, 11–13 days by the female; fledging, 12–16 days. One or two broods, one in the North.

Read: Brewer, R., "Comparative Notes on the Life History of the Carolina Chickadee," *Wilson Bulletin 73* (1961): 348–373. Odum, E. P., "Annual Cycle of the Black-capped Chickadee," *Auk 58* (1941): 314–333.

TUFTED TITMOUSE. 164. *Parus bicolor*. Common resident in wet woodlands in e. U.S. north to Iowa, s. Ontario, s. New York, often visiting woodland-bordering gardens.

Its food preferences are similar to the chickadees', favoring a wide variety of nut meats, acorns and larger seeds; in warm weather caterpillars form a substantial part of the diet. Titmice will be attracted to the feeding trays by bread, cracked nuts, peanut butter mix, suet and sunflower seeds. They will use a swinging feeder, as well as an enclosed table.

Nesting is in a tree hole or an old woodpecker nest, but titmice will occupy a bluebird-type standard box placed 4–5 feet high against a tree trunk in the woods. The entrance hole of 1¼–1½-inch diameter should be 6–8 inches above a 4-inch square floor. Titmice often gather hair, wool and other fluffy material to line their nests, and will use any such materials put out where they can find them.

4–5 eggs, white with brown speckles, early April–late May. Incubation, 12–14 days; fledging, 15–16 days. One or two broods.

Read: Gillespie, M., "Behavior and local distribution of the Tufted Titmouse in winter and spring," *Bird Banding 1* (1930): 113–127. Bent, A. C., *Bulletin 191:* 393–408.

WHITE-BREASTED NUTHATCH. 164. *Sitta carolinensis.* Common resident throughout our area north to s. Canada. Found almost anywhere there are trees: woodlands, orchard, town parks and gardens.

Nuthatches feed by hitching themselves up (or down) the trunks

of trees, searching for insect food in the bark. They come readily to the winter bird table for bread, melon seeds, nutmeats, sunflower seeds, hemp and especially suet.

Nesting is normally in tree holes, but a bird box similar to that for the timouse, but a little deeper (8–10 inches) and placed in the same situation, 5–20 feet above ground, may be tenanted.

5–9 white eggs speckled with red-brown are laid from mid-April to late May. Incubation, 12–15 days by female; fledging, about 23–25 days. One brood.

Read: Bent, A. C., "Life Histories of North American Nuthatches, Wrens, Thrushes and their allies." *U.S. National Museum Bulletin 195* (1948): 1–14.

RED-BREASTED NUTHATCH. 164. *Sitta canadensis.* A migratory nuthatch, wintering in our area from s. Canada south to the Gulf of Mexico and n. Florida. Breeds from Newfoundland and s. Canada south into the higher Appalachians.

A bird primarily of coniferous forests, the Red-breasted feeds in typical nuthatch fashion, gleaning insects from the bark of trees. It will patronize the bird table set with nutmeats, sunflower seeds and suet.

Nests in tree holes, but will sometimes tenant a nestbox, preferably in the hollow log style, with an entrance one inch in diameter, set 6–8 inches above a 3-inch square floor. The box should be placed against a tree trunk, 5–20 feet high, in the woods. This little bird will coat the entrance with pitch.

Eggs, 5–6, white with reddish spots, early May–late June. Incubation, 12–14 days; fledging, 18–21 days. Normally one brood.

Read: Bent, A. C., *Bulletin 15* (1948): 22–44.

BROWN-HEADED NUTHATCH. 165. *Sitta pusilla.* A bird of the southern pine woods, resident from Arkansas to Delaware, south to the Gulf coast.

Food and nesting habits closely similar to that of the Red-breasted Nuthatch, but the eggs are more heavily spotted, and egg dates are a month earlier. Non-migratory.

Read: Bent, A. C., *Bulletin 195* (1948): 35–44.

BROWN CREEPER. 165. *Certhia familiaris.* Widespread woodland species, common in migration, breeding from n. U.S. to mid-Canada, south in Appalachians to North Carolina. Winters from n. U.S. south to Gulf coast.

Feeds on insects on the trunks and larger limbs of trees, creeping upward with the aid of its stiff tail feathers. Its choice food is arthropods, but it will be attracted to peanut butter mix, or suet smeared into the bark of a tree on the woodland edge.

Nesting is in cavities under the bark of trees, particularly in balsam fir.

4–6 white eggs, marked with brownish dots. Egg dates, early May–mid-July. Incubation, 11–12 days; fledging, 13–14 days. One or two broods.

Read: Bent, A. C., *Bulletin 195:* 56–71.

HOUSE WREN. 165. *Troglodytes aedon.* This is the sound of summer in our area, a welcome bird in any garden. Widespread in parks, orchards, suburban gardens and rural areas where it darts from brush to thicket to hedgerow. Breeds from n. Texas and

Georgia north to mid-Canada. Winters from Florida and the Gulf coast south into Mexico.

House Wrens feed entirely on animal food—insects and other arthropods.

They nest in holes in trees, under the eaves of buildings, in drain pipes and a wide variety of cavities, including bird boxes. (See illustration on page 23). Houses should be hung in a shady spot, from a tree or building, from 5–10 feet high. Since wrens are territorial, one pair per average garden is the maximum, but since the female is choosy about nesting sites, often a choice of several boxes may encourage occupancy. Multiple trial nests, whether for practice, decoys or enticement, are built.

The eggs, pinkish-white, dotted with brown, often almost solid brown in color, 5–12 to a clutch, normally 6–8. Eggs, mid-May–late June. Incubation, 13 days; fledging, 12–18 days. Two broods.

Read: Bent, A. C., *Bulletin 195:* 113–146.

WINTER WREN. 168. *Troglodytes troglodytes.* This is "The Wren" or Jenny Wren, of Britain, not quite as domesticated in the New World, a tiny mite to be saddled with that cave man tag. Breeds from Newfoundland and mid-Canada south to n. U.S. southward in higher mountains to Georgia. Winters from Nebraska and Massachusetts south to mid-Florida and the Gulf coast. A denizen of brush piles, wet woodland underbrush, especially near water. A marvelous singer on its breeding grounds.

Feeds on small insects and other arthropods, snails, worms.

Nests low to the ground, near water, in a hole in a stump or the roots of an overturned log. Said to nest in House Wren boxes; perhaps these should be placed in a woodpile or vine-covered wall.

Eggs white, 5–6, spotted brownish red. Egg dates, May–July. Incubation, probably 14–16 days; fledging, 16–17 days. Usually two broods.

Read: Armstrong, E. A., *The Wren,* London: Collins, (1955). Bent, A. C., *Bulletin 195:* 148–176.

BEWICK'S WREN. 168. *Thryomanes bewickii.* A shy, uncommon and local summer resident in brush and thickets from central Pennsylvania, s. Michigan and s. Iowa south to central Oklahoma and Texas, central Alabama and n. Georgia. Winters mainly in southern states from Gulf coast and n. Florida north to South Carolina, Kentucky, central Arkansas.

Food and nesting habits similar to the House Wren. Nest-box and bird table requirements the same.

Eggs, 5–7, white dotted with reddish brown or other colors, early April–late July. Incubation, 14 days; fledging, 14 days. Two or three broods.

Read: Miller, E. V., "Behavior of the Bewick's Wren," *Condor 43* (1941): 81–99. Bent, A. C., *Bulletin 195:* 176–186.

CAROLINA WREN. 168. *Thryothorus ludovicianus.* Common in brush and thickets from New Jersey, Ohio, and s. Nebraska south to the Gulf. Rare and local resident north of its normal range.

Food is similar to that of the House Wren, and Carolinas will come to the bird feeder for peanut butter mix, nutmeats, suet and raw hamburger.

Nesting is in cavities of all kinds, both natural and man-provided; in trees, in the roots of upturned trees, in tin cans, coffee pots, old hats, pockets of clothing left hanging in outbuildings, and in nest boxes. Boxes should be placed against a sheltered wall or tree, 5–10 feet high. An entrance 1¼-inches by 2½-inches should be 6–8 inches above a floor 4-inches square. A woven basket 8-inches deep, placed under an eave, may also be favored.

4–6 creamy white eggs spotted with reddish brown are laid. Egg dates, early April–late July. Incubation, 12–14 days; fledging, 12–14 days. 2–3 broods.

Read: Bent, A. C., *Bulletin 195:* 205–218.

MOCKINGBIRD. 170. *Mimus polyglottos.* Common resident throughout our area north to s. New England, Ohio, s. Iowa and Nebraska, with scattered breeding locations in Massachusetts, Maine and Nova Scotia. Common around towns and cities where its vocalization, often nocturnal, makes it a part of American folklore.

Almost omnivorous, feeding on animal life mainly in warm weather, including insects, snails, lizards and worms, but taking fruit and berries in all seasons, particularly in the colder months. The Mocker will be attracted to the bird garden by plantings of fruiting shrubs and vines. At the bird feeder, it prefers dried fruits such as raisins and currants, suet and nutmeats.

Nests in dense shrubbery, hedges, trees and vines, often close to the house, from 3–10 feet high.

Eggs, 3–6, are varied in color, usually bluish or greenish-white, heavily marked with brown. April to July. Incubation, average 12 days; fledging, about 12 days. Two broods.

Read: Michener, H. and I. R., "Mockingbirds, their territories and individualities," *Condor 37* (1935) : 97–140. Bent, A. C., *Bulletin 195* (1948) : 295–320.

CATBIRD. 170. *Dumetella carolinensis.* Abundant summer resident in parks, suburban gardens, rural areas and woodlands from s. Canada south to n. Gulf states. Winters in s. U.S., but frequently lingers in sheltered thickets or near feeding stations n. to New England and s. Michigan.

Preferred food is the fleshy fruit of berries of all kinds, but in season insects and other animal fare is taken. Catbirds are attracted to plantings of berry-bearing shrubs and vines, and will come to the winter feeder for raisins, grapes, berries, suet, bread, cheese and nutmeats.

Nesting in dense thickets and hedges, 2–10 feet high, often close to water. Eggs, 2–5 bluish-green. Early May–late June. Incubation, 12–13 days; fledging, 12–13 days. One or two broods.

Read: Gabrielson, I. N., "Nest Life of the Catbird," *Wilson Bulletin 25* (1913) : 166–187. Bent, A. C., *Bulletin 195* (1948) : 320–351.

BROWN THRASHER. 170. *Toxostoma rufum.* Abundant, widespread breeding bird in open woodland, parkland and brushy country from n. U.S. and southernmost Canada southward in our area to the Gulf. Winters in s. U.S., but frequently lingers in the northern states in sheltered locations.

Food preferences similar to the Catbird, with perhaps more emphasis on animal food. The Brown Thrasher is attracted in summer to the garden by the same plantings and in winter by the same foods as the Catbird. Thrashers are enthusiastic patrons of the bird bath.

Nesting is on the ground in thickets or thorny tangles or in shrubbery, from 2–7 feet high, rarely higher.

Eggs, 4–5, pale blue, marked with brownish. Early April–late June. Incubation, 11–14 days; fledging, 10–13 days. Two broods.

Read: Thomas, Ruth, *Crip Come Home,* (New York: Harper & Bros.), 1952. Gabrielson, I. N., "A study of the home life of the Brown Thrasher," *Wilson Bulletin 24* (1912) : 65–91. Bent, A. C., *Bulletin 195: 351–375.*

ROBIN. 171. *Turdus migratorius*. Familiar, abundant summer resident in city parks, suburbs, rural areas and woodland edge to northern limit of trees in Canada, south to n. areas of Gulf states. Winters in the South, but is found in some numbers in northern states where shelter and food are available.

Feeds on fields, golf courses, lawns, etc., for earthworms and other invertebrates in season, and on a wide variety of berries and fruits. Attracted to the well-kept, unsterilized lawn and to the bird feeder stocked with raisins, cut-up fruit, bread and water.

Nesting is on a tree branch or crotch or under an eave, or on a nesting platform provided for it. (See illustration on page 17.) Place it under an eave or against a tree, from 8–16 feet high, in the shade.

Eggs, 3–5, normally four, are "robin's egg blue," naturally. Mid-April–late July. Incubation, 11–13 days; fledging, 12–14 days. Two or three broods.

Read: Bent, A. C., "Life Histories of North American Thrushes, Kinglets, and their Allies," *U.S. National Museum Bulletin 196* (1949) : 14–66. Howell, J. C., "Notes on the nesting of the American Robin," *American Midland Naturalist 28* (1942) : 529–603. Schwartz, W. E., "A detailed study of a family of Robins," *Wilson Bulletin 51* (1939) : 157–169.

WOOD THRUSH. 171. *Hylocichla mustelina*. A common, vocally eloquent resident of the deciduous forest floor, from n. U.S. and extreme s. Canada almost to the Gulf. Winters very rarely north of Florida, south to Panama.

Food is mainly animal (insects and other arthropods and worms) in spring, increasingly vegetable in summer and colder months, with fruits and berries of many kinds included. You may attract Wood Thrushes to the woodland-bordering garden with fruiting shrubs and a bird bath. It occasionally comes to the bird table for suet, peanut butter mix, berries and bread.

Nesting, like the Robin, is in a tree, 5–15 feet high, in rare instances on the ground. The eggs, 3–4, are greenish-blue. Late April–mid-July. Incubation, 13 days by female; fledging, 12–14 days. Two broods.

Read: Bent, A. C., *Bulletin 196* (1949) : 101–123.

EASTERN BLUEBIRD. 173. *Sialia sialis*. Beloved roadside, orchard and open woodland summer resident, rarely common, from s.

Canada to Gulf throughout our area. Retreats from northern areas in winter, occasionally wintering along the coast north to New England.

Natural food is mainly animal in summer, including arthropods and small invertebrates. In colder weather, fruits and berries of many kinds are taken. For the bird table, provide raisins, currants and other food at a stationary feeder. A shallow bird bath and a fertile lawn may attract bluebirds, as will such shrubs as coton-easters, pyracantha, viburnums, mulberry, bayberry and sumach.

Bluebirds traditionally nest in tree holes, especially in old apple trees, but they are the most grateful tenants of bird boxes. A consistent program of nestbox placement can markedly increase the population in rural areas. Boxes (see illustration on page 23) are widely available commercially. They should be placed on posts five feet high, early in the spring, in groups of three, each group ¼-mile from the next.

Eggs 3–6, pale blue, rarely white. Mid-March–mid-July. Incubation, 12–16 days: fledging, 15–18 days. Two or three broods, often in different nests.

Read: Thomas, R. T., "A Study of Eastern Bluebirds in Arkansas," *Wilson Bulletin 58* (1946): 143–183. Hartshorne, J. M., "Behavior of the Eastern Bluebird at the Nest," *The Living Bird I* (1962): 137–149. (Ithaca, N.Y.: Cornell Laboratory of Ornithology). Bent, A. C., *Bulletin 196:* 233–260.

CEDAR WAXWING. 176. *Bombycilla cedrorum.* Common but irregular resident from mid-Province latitudes to North Carolina,

Georgia, Kansas. Winters throughout the area, north roughly to the U.S.-Canada border. This gentle, gregarious bird wanders almost anywhere in woodlands, open areas, parks and gardens.

Waxwings are voracious feeders on fruits and berries of all kinds. In warm weather they may take many caterpillars and other insect life, often "flycatching" in flight. They will be attracted to the garden planted for fruits and berries, by bird baths and by berries, raisins and cut-up fruit at the feeder.

Nest, in open woodland, a loosely made cup 6–35 feet high.

Eggs, 3–6, blue-gray spotted with black. A late nester, with egg from early June–late September. Incubation, 12–16 days; fledging, about 16–18 days. One or two broods.

Read: Putnam, L. S., "Life History of the Cedar Waxwing," *Wilson Bulletin 61* (1949): 141–182. Bent, A. C., "Life Histories of North American Wagtails, Shrikes, Vireos and their Allies," *U.S. National Museum Bulletin 197* (1950): 79–102.

STARLING. 177. *Sturnus vulgaris.* Abundant, ubiquitous introduced resident throughout our area north to mid-Provinces, flocking in large roosts in winter.

The Starling forages on the ground and in trees, even hawking for insects on the wing. Takes animal and vegetable food of almost any kind, combing the lawn for grubs, hacking out fruit in the trees, gluttonous at the bird feeder, especially liking suet.

Nests in tree holes, building cavities, nestboxes, often in colonies. Will drive out more desirable native birds such as woodpeckers, bluebirds, Purple Martins. Sometimes they can be discouraged by swinging or enclosed feeders, or bird box entrances no larger than 1½-inches in diameter.

Eggs, 5–7, pale blue. Mid-March–September. Incubation, 12–14 days; fledging, 20–22 days. Two broods, sometimes three.

Read: Bent, A. C., *Bulletin 197* (1950): 182–214.

PROTHONOTARY WARBLER. 185. *Protonotaria citrea.* The "golden swamp warbler" is a summer resident in wooded swamps and river bottoms from central New York and Wisconsin south to the Gulf and central Florida.

Its food is entirely animal: flies, ants, bees, snails and aquatic invertebrates.

The Prothonotary is the only warbler in our area that will nest in a bird house (or tin can, pail, mailbox, coat pocket, etc.). A rustic box with an entrance 1½-inches in diameter, five inches above a 4-inch square floor, hung 5–7 feet high against a tree over water, just may attract a pair, if you are lucky enough to have such a location. Several boxes should be hung since the male often makes dummy nests.

Eggs, 3–8 (normally 5–6), rose-cream spotted with lavender and brown. Mid-April–late June. Incubation, 12–14 days; fledging, 11 days. Two broods.

Read: Walkinshaw, L. H., "The Prothonotary Warbler in Tennessee and Michigan," *Wilson Bulletin 53* (1941): 3–21. Griscom, L., and A. Sprunt, Jr., *The Warblers of North America,* (New York: Devin-Adair), 1957. 46–49. Bent, A. C., "Life Histories of North American Wood Warblers," *U.S. National Museum Bulletin 203* (1953): 17–30.

PINE WARBLER. 201. *Dendroica pinus.* Summer resident in open pine woods from s. Canada to Gulf states and Florida. Winters in s. U.S. north to s. Illinois and Virginia.

Food normally insects, but in winter will come to the bird feeder for bread, corn meal, peanut butter mix, nutmeats and especially suet. It will also take berries such as sumac, ivy, grape and bayberry.

Nests in pine trees, to 135 feet, but usually 10–25 feet high.

Eggs 4–5, white with brown spots. Late March–July. Incubation, probably about 14–15 days; fledging, probably 10 days.

Other warblers that will come to the bird table in winter include the ORANGE-CROWNED WARBLER, *Vermivora celata,* for bread, suet, nutmeats; the MYRTLE WARBLER, *Dendroica coronata,* for suet, nutmeats, berries, the BLACK-THROATED BLUE WARBLER, *Dendroica caerulescens,* for bread, and the YELLOW-THROATED WARBLER, *Dendroica dominica,* for cornmeal.

Read: Bent, A. C., *Bulletin 203,* and Griscom-Sprunt, entire volumes.

HOUSE SPARROW. 209. *Passer domesticus.* Introduced from Europe, an abundant resident in cities, towns and around farms throughout the area, north to the tree line in Canada.

The House Sparrow is one of the scalawags of the bird world, an avian pig around the bird table, operating an ornithological mafia that bullies smaller birds. Prefers seeds of all kinds and bread. May be discouraged somewhat by swinging feeders, and sometimes generous bribes of stale bread on the ground will divert the House Sparrow from feeding trays. Many bird gardeners trap and eliminate this rogue, but others pay the price (doubled) and noisy brawls for the company of this intelligent rascal.

At nesting time the House Sparrow is even more detrimental, usurping nesting sites from bluebirds, Purple Martins and other cavity-nesting species. Nests also in ivy and crevices in buildings.

Eggs, 4–8, shades of white with brown or other speckles. February–July. Incubation, 12–13 days by female; fledging, 14–16 days. Two or more broods.

Read: Bent. A. C., "Life Histories of North American Blackbirds, Orioles, Tanagers and their Allies," *U.S. National Museum Bulletin 211* (1958): 1–24. Wing L., "Spread of the Starling and English Sparrow," *Auk 60:* 74–87. Kalmbach, E. R., "Economic Status of the English Sparrow," *U.S. Dept. of Agric. Tech. Bulletin 711* (1940).

EASTERN MEADOWLARK. 210. *Sturnella magna.* Common summer resident in open fields and farm lands throughout the book area north to mid-Canada. Replaced in mid-continent (east to w. New York) by the similar WESTERN MEADOWLARK, 210, *Sturnella neglecta,* a more melodious singer. Winters roughly from U.S.-Canadian border southward in increasing numbers.

The Meadowlark feeds mainly on insects and other invertebrate animal life, supplementing this diet in cold weather with a variety of grain and grass seeds. Will patronize the bird feeder in the field-bordering garden for cracked corn, millet and other seeds. A common "lawn gleaner" in Florida in winter. It is attracted to lawn sprinklers.

Nests on the ground under a canopy of living grasses.

Eggs, 3–7 (average five) are white spotted with brown. Early April–early July. Incubation, 14 days; fledging, 11–12 days.

Read: Lanyon, W. E., *The Comparative Biology of the Meadowlarks in Wisconsin.* (Boston: Publ. Nuttall Ornith. Club No. 1), 1958. Bent, A. C., *Bulletin 211* (1958): 53–99.

RED-WINGED BLACKBIRD. 211. *Agelaius phoeniceus.* Abundant, widespread resident in marshes, swamps, meadows and woodlands near water, from mid-Provinces south through our area. In winter moves into southern states, often concentrating in tremendous roosts, uncommon north of New Jersey, Ohio, s. Illinois, Kansas.

Omnivorous in warmer months, turning to grains, seeds and berries in autumn and winter. Comes to the feeder for bread, seeds, grains. In summer mulberries and other fruiting plants will attract this handsome blackbird.

Nests in colonies, in grass tussocks or bushes to five feet high.

Eggs, 3–5 bluish-green with dark markings. Mid-April–late June. Incubation, 12 days; fledging, 11 days. Two or three broods.

Read: Allen, A. A., "The Red-winged Blackbird, a study of the ecology of a cat-tail marsh." *Proceedings, Linnaean Society of N.Y. 24–25* (1914) : 43–128. Bent, A. C., *Bulletin 211:* 123–156.

ORCHARD ORIOLE. 211. *Icterus spurius.* Summer resident, locally common in orchards, groves, around farms from Gulf coast and Florida north to Massachusetts, Great Lakes, South Dakota. Winters south of the U.S., leaving early—often by mid-July.

Food is mostly animal, but it also feeds on berries, fruit-tree blossoms and nectar. A bird with a "sweet tooth," it occasionally comes to a hummingbird feeder for syrup, or to the feeder for bread spread with jelly.

Nests in groves and orchards, in loose colonies, in a variety of trees or shrubs, in nests from 6–70 feet high.

The eggs, 4–6 in number, are pale bluish white, with darker markings. Mid-May–mid-June. Incubation, 12–15 days; fledging, 11–14 days. One brood.

Read, Bent, A. C., *Bulletin 211:* 191–210.

BALTIMORE ORIOLE. 211. *Icterus galbula.* Summer resident in parks, suburban and rural areas, along roads, where tall trees provide nesting sites, often over water. Breeding range is from mid-Provinces south to northern parts of Gulf States. Winters south of the U.S., occasionally lingering at northern feeding stations.

Omnivorous, feeding on insects and other arthropods and invertebrates as well as fruits and berries. Comes to the feeder for nutmeats, suet, orange slices, sugar syrup. Also attracted to the bird garden by berry-bearing plants, colorful knitting wools for nest-weaving, and water in summer.

Nest is pendant, often high in American elms over roads or water, 25–60 feet up.

The eggs, 4–6, are pale gray, darkly marked. Late May–mid-June. Incubation, 12–14 days; fledging, 11–14 days. One brood.

Read: Bent, A. C., *Bulletin 211:* 247–270.

BOAT-TAILED GRACKLE. 213. *Cassidix mexicanus.* Largest black-bird in our area, resident from s. Florida and w. Texas north to s. Jersey, near salt water, but inland in Florida. A bird of coastal marsh and town and along inland streams.

Feeds on arthropods, small fish, frogs, lizards and smaller mammals, and (more in winter) on corn, rice, grain and grass seeds. Will occasionally visit the feeding trays for bread, corn, meat scraps, preferring to take food on the ground.

Nesting, often in loose colonies, in cattail, cordgrass, wax myrtle and taller trees such as willow, close to water.

Usually there are three eggs (2–5) blue or grayish blue marked with black or brown. Early March–mid June. Incubation, 13–14 days by female; fledging, 20–23 days. Two broods.

Read, Bent, A. C., *Bulletin 211:* 335–374.

COMMON GRACKLE. 213. *Quiscalus quiscula.* Abundant and apparently increasing summer resident in rural areas, suburbs, parks and swamps throughout our area north to mid-Provinces. Winters from New York, Ohio and Kansas southward.

Virtually omnivorous, taking animal and plant food alike in warmer months, mostly plant food in colder months—nuts, grains, seeds, acorns, berries and larger fruits. Comes regularly to the bird feeder, where it is high on the pecking order. It will take almost anything offered: bread, corn, nutmeats, grains, sunflower seeds, suet. In summer it often forages on the fertile lawn. The grackle, however, is a character of questionable repute. It is known to ravage the nests of smaller birds, and at the bird table will attack and occasionally kill smaller competition.

The nesting is colonial, in dense trees, evergreens preferred, especially near water. The nest can be almost any height.

Eggs, 4–6, are variable in color, pale green to light brown, with darker markings. Early April–mid-June. Incubation, 14 days; fledging, 14–18 days. One or two broods.

Read: Bent, A. C., *Bulletin 211:* 374–421.

BROWN-HEADED COWBIRD. 216. *Molothrus ater.* Abundant summer resident in a wide variety of habitats from mid-South states to mid-Canadian provinces Winters mainly in southern states (often in large flocks), but is found uncommonly in s. New England and northern states.

Food is a wide variety of animal and plant life, particularly small seeds and grains. It is a persistent visitor to the bird feeder for these foods.

Cowbirds parasitize other species by laying their eggs in nests not of their own building. They are undesirable intruders, since the young cowbirds are usually larger and faster-growing than the host nestlings, thus dominating the food supply. Often the death of the other nestlings results. Over 150 species have been victimized by this method. Occasionally, too, the adult cowbird destroys or eats the eggs of the host species

Eggs, 4–5, are pale gray with darker spots, laid one, two or rarely three per nest. Late April–mid-July. Incubation, 11–14 days; fledging, 11 days. One brood.

Read: Friedmann, H., *The Cowbirds,* Springfield, Illinois: Chas. C Thomas, (1929). Hann, H. W., "Cowbird at the nest," *Wilson Bulletin 53* (1941): 211–221. Bent, A. C., *Bulletin 211* (1958): 421–455.

CARDINAL. 220. *Richmondena cardinalis.* Throughout the book area north to the northern states, s. Ontario and s. New England this is an abundant resident. Inhabits gardens, bushy thickets, hedgerows and scrubby woodlands.

Food is both animal and vegetable in warm months, mainly vegetable in winter, including more than 100 kinds of seeds, grains, nuts, berries and fruits. A welcome and attractive patron of the bird table, often the earliest to arrive in the morning. Will visit swinging or platform feeders for bread, corn, small seeds, nutmeats, peanut butter mix and sunflower seeds. May be encouraged to nest by the presence of hedges or thickets of dense shrubbery or vines.

Nest is 6–8 feet high in a bush or vine. Eggs, 3–4, are greenish or whitish. Early April–late July. Incubation, 12 days; fledging, 10–11 days. Two or three broods.

Read: Bent, A. C., "Life Histories of North American Cardinals, Grosbeaks, Buntings, etc." *U.S. National Museum Bulletin 237, Part 1* (1968): 1–25.

BLACK-HEADED GROSBEAK 221. *Pheucticus melanocephalus.* A bird of the West which is a very rare autumn-winter visitant to northeastern coastal areas. It occasionally lingers where the bird feeder provides sunflower and other seeds, white bread and butter.

Read: Bent, A. C., *Bulletin 237, Part 1* (1968): 55–67.

BLUE GROSBEAK. 221. *Guiraca caerulea.* Locally common resident in southern states north to Maryland, Illinois and Nebraska, occasionally appearing on the northeastern coast in autumn. Winters in Central America. A bird of scrub, thicket, grain fields and rural roadsides.

Omnivorous, favoring blackberries, grain and small seeds, as well as large insects and other arthropods. The bird table set with sunflower seeds, sorghum and other grain sometimes attracts it.

Nests in thick shrubbery, tall weeds, low trees; nest 3–13 feet high.

Eggs, 3–4, are bluish white. Late April–late June. Incubation, 12–14 days; fledging, said to be 9 days. Two broods.

Read: Bent, A. C., *Bulletin 237, Part 1* (1968) : 67–78.

INDIGO BUNTING. 222. *Passerina cyanea.* Common summer resident in rural areas, fields, margins of woodlands, often seen along roads on telephone wires, throughout our area n. to U.S.-Canadian border and s. Ontario and New Brunswick. Winters south of the U.S.

Food is mainly vegetable, including berries such as blackberry and mulberry, but mostly grain and grass seeds. Some animal food is taken. Indigo Buntings like the bird bath in hot weather, and come to the bird feeder for peanut and other nutmeats, cracked corn and wheat.

Nesting is 1–3 feet up in the crotch of a bush or shrub in dense cover.

Eggs, 3–4, pale blue with darker markings. Early May–late June. Incubation, 12–13 days; fledging, 10 days. One or two broods.

Read: Bent, A. C., *Bulletin 237, Part 1* (1968) : 80–111.

PAINTED BUNTING. 222. *Passerina ciris.* This little avian gem is a summer resident around the Gulf of Mexico, north to Kansas and s. North Carolina. Winters in s. Louisiana and Florida. A thicket dweller that feeds on arthropods, snails, grass and weed seeds. It comes to the feeder in Florida for cracked corn and bread crumbs.

Nests in low bushes or lower branches of tall trees, often in Spanish moss.

Eggs, 3–4, white spotted with brown. Mid-May–mid-July. Incubation, 10–12 days; fledging, 12–14 days. Three or four broods.

Read: Bent, A. C., *Bulletin 237, Part 1* (1968): 137–155.

DICKCISSEL. 223. *Spiza americana.* Abundant bird of fields, meadows and prairies of the Mississippi River basin, found increasingly in autumn and winter along the Eastern seaboard n. to Massachusetts.

Its food is largely animal—arthropods and other small invertebrates of many species—but it also eats small grain and grass seeds in winter. Dickcissels come to the bird table for small seeds, grain and peanut butter mix. Often, in the East, they associate with flocks of mixed sparrows or House Sparrows, which they resemble.

Nest is on the ground in a grass clump, or in a small bush or tree as high as 15 feet.

The eggs, 3–5, are pale blue. Mid-May–early July. Incubation, 12–13 days by female; fledging, 10–11 days.

Read: Bent, A. C., *Bulletin 237, Part 1* (1968): 158–191.

EVENING GROSBEAK. 223. *Hesperiphona vespertina.* Striking, noisy breeding bird of northern evergreen forests from mid-Province latitudes south to n. Minnesota, Michigan, New York and New England. Flocks wander erratically in winter south to Arkansas, Tennessee and recently to Florida.

In summer the Evening Grosbeak feeds on buds, berries, seeds and small arthropods. In colder months it is partial to the seeds of many trees and shrubs, especially the box elder, sugar maple and ash-leaved maple. Flocks often become "dependent" on the bird table, frequently returning year after year to feeders where sunflower, hemp, safflower and peanuts are provided. A voracious and expensive guest. Also attracted by salt-soaked earth.

Nests in conifer or broad-leaved trees, near the tip of a branch 20–60 feet high.

Eggs, 3–4, are blue-green with dark markings. June–late July. Incubation, 13–14 days; fledging, 12–14 days.

Read: Bent, A. C., *Bulletin 237, Part 1* (1968): 206–256.

PURPLE FINCH. 223. *Carpodacus purpureus.* Common but local summer resident in towns, suburbs, open woodlands and rural areas from the tree line in Canada south to n. U.S. In winter it moves southward in flocks, may be found almost anywhere in the book area from s. Canada to n. Florida.

Purple Finches feed almost entirely on fruits and seeds, but they will also take buds, flowers, nutmeats and insects. At the bird feeder, nutmeats, honey syrup, corn bread, safflower seeds, sunflower seeds, squash, pumpkin and hemp seeds attract them.

Nest is usually 5–60 feet high in a tall evergreen or in a deciduous shrub.

The eggs, 4–6, are blue with brown markings at the larger end. Mid-May–late June. Incubation, 13 days; fledging, 14 days. One brood.

Read: Bent, A. C., *Bulletin 237, Part 1* (1968) : 264–278.

HOUSE FINCH. 238W. *Carpodacus mexicanus.* Western species that appeared in the East (Long Island) in 1941, probably released captive birds, and has spread to include a breeding range from s. New England to s. New York and New Jersey. Wanders southward in winter, reported from central New York to North Carolina.

A bird of park and garden, favoring locations where ornamental evergreens have been planted.

Feeds largely on seeds, but also takes buds and fruits of trees and shrubs. Will come to the feeder for a variety of small seeds, and to the bird bath in summer.

Nests in a wide variety of locations, often in a low evergreen, often around buildings and man-made objects (flower baskets, etc.).

Eggs, 4–5 blue-green, spotted with dark markings. Mid-April–July. Incubation, 12–14 days; fledging, 14–16 days. Two to three broods.

Read: Miller, L., "The Biography of Nip and Tuck," *Condor* 23 (1921): 41–47. Bent, A. C., *Bulletin 237, Part 1* (1968): 290–322.

PINE SISKIN. 225. *Spinus pinus.* Breeds in conifer forests of n. Canada and n. U.S., also mountains of North Carolina. Winter range is entire book area, but it is unpredictable in appearance. Rare in s. Florida.

The siskin is a gregarious wanderer, often associating in large flocks with goldfinches, redpolls and crossbills.

In summer the siskin feeds on buds, leaves, insects and seeds. In winter its food is largely weed and conifer seeds. It will be attracted by cone-bearing trees, and occasionally to the feeding trays where it will take millet, sunflower, hemp and other small seeds and cracked butternuts.

Nest is always in a conifer, 10–20 feet above the ground.

Eggs, 3–4, are pale blue with dark spots. March–August. Incubation, 12–14 days by the female; fledging, 13–15 days. One brood annually, possibly two.

Read: Bent, A. C., *Bulletin 237, Part 1* (1968) : 424–447.

AMERICAN GOLDFINCH. 335. *Spinus tristis*. Breeds from the mountains of Georgia and Alabama and s. Oklahoma north to the southern Provinces. Winters almost throughout the area.

One of the most attractive and conspicuous finches, a common bird of woodland edge and weedy field, open country and suburban garden. It is found in flocks almost year round, often, in winter, with other wandering finches.

The goldfinch is a consumer of weed and flower seeds, but in warm months its diet includes some insects and succulent plant growth. It will occasionally drop in at the winter bird table for seeds and nutmeats, but it is better attracted by seedheads of garden flowers and weeds left standing and by birch and alder catkins.

The nest is normally in a low tree or shrub within a few feet of the ground (but up to 45 feet rarely).

Five (4–6) eggs, pale blue, are laid. Early July–mid-September. Incubation, 12–14 days by female; fledging, 11–15 days. One or two broods.

Read: Stokes, A. W., "Breeding behavior of the Goldfinch," *Wilson Bulletin 62* (1950): 112–125. Nickell, W. P., "Studies of Habitats, Territory, and Nests of the Eastern Goldfinch," *Auk 68* (1951): 447–470. Bent, A. C., *Bulletin 237, Part 1* (1968): 447–469.

RED CROSSBILL. 228. *Loxia curvirostra*. Breeds in the spruce forests of Canada and n. U.S. south into the Appalachians. Appears erratically throughout the area in winter, to the southern states.

It is a rare and red-letter day when the handsome crossbills visit the bird feeder for sunflower seeds or the evergreen border for cone seeds. This wanderer mainly inhabits evergreen forests and groves, using its uniquely adapted bill to pry open cones, but it also feeds on weed seeds, fruits, and in summer on a variety of arthropods.

Nest is high on the south side of evergreens.

Eggs, 3–4, greenish-white, marked with purple-red. January–June. Incubation, 12–14 days; fledging, 17–20 days. One brood, possibly two.

Read: Bailey, A. M., et al., "The Red Crossbills of Colorado," *Museum Pictorial 9,* (1953), Denver Museum of Natural History. Bent, A. C., *Bulletin 237, Part 1* (1968) : 500–526.

WHITE-WINGED CROSSBILL. 228. *Loxia leucoptera.* Has roughly the same range, but not wandering as far southward in winter, and the same habits as the Red Crossbill. It is rarely seen at the bird feeder.

Read: Bent, A. C., *Bulletin 237, Part 1* (1968): 527–544.

RUFOUS-SIDED TOWHEE. 229. *Pipilo erythrophthalmus.* Breeds roughly from U.S.-Canadian border south through book area. Winters from mid-Atlantic latitudes southward, and rarely in sheltered gardens and thickets in the north. Its habitat is varied: dry and open woodlands, brushy second growth, parks and overgrown garden borders—wherever there is thick cover. The towhee is a ground feeder, taking about half vegetable half animal matter. Towhees will come to the bird feeder for crumbs, peanuts and nutmeats, seeds and wheat scattered on the ground near cover. A reliable source of food provided near shrubbery will often induce nesting.

The nest is on the ground, concealed in leaves or debris, occasionally up to five feet high in a bush.

Eggs, 4–6, are pale blue-green, spotted with brown. April–July. Incubation, 12–13 days; fledging, 10–12 days. Two broods.

Read: Barbour, R. W., "Observations of the breeding habits of the Red-eyed Towhee," *American Midland Naturalist 45* (1951): 672–678. Bent, A. C., *Bulletin 237, Part 1* (1968): 562–602.

SLATE-COLORED JUNCO. 234. *Junco hyemalis.* Breeds from the tree limit in Canada south to the northern states and at high altitudes south to Georgia. Winters from s. Canada south throughout the area except peninsular Florida and w. Texas.

An abundant bird of conifer forest, clearing and woodland roadside, found in winter in open woodland, brushy fields and landscaped areas, including sheltered gardens.

It consumes seeds of trees and weeds primarily, but includes a variety of plant foods and, in its summer diet, some animal food. A handsome, gregarious and musical visitor to the bird table, preferring to feed on the ground. Scatter small grain seeds, cracked corn, sunflower seeds, peanut hearts and even suet.

The nest is low to the ground, under an overhanging bank or roots of a fallen tree or in a brush pile.

Eggs, 4–5, are pale green with brown spots. Early May–July. Incubation, 12 days by female; fledging, 12–13 days. Two broods.

Read: Bent, A. C., *Bulletin 237, Part 2* (1968): 1029–1050. Occasionally in the East, the dark headed, brown-backed OREGON JUNCO 234., *Junco oreganus,* may appear at the winter feeder. Its food preferences are the same as those of *hyemalis.*

TREE SPARROW. 235. *Spizella arborea.* Breeds in the far north, beyond the tree limit south to mid-Canada; found in winter throughout the book area from mid-Canada south to mid-U.S. latitudes, farther south in the southwest.

In winter travels in flocks, varying in abundance from place to place and winter to winter, but always frequenting open woodlands, farm fields, parklands and gardens. Often our most abundant wintering sparrow.

Feeds on grass, weed and grain seeds on the ground and in the seedpod, taking the usual quota of arthropods in the warm months. A welcome and dainty visitor to the bird table (preferring the ground) where it takes all kinds of small seeds, cornmeal and grain.

Read: Bent, A. C., *Bulletin 237, Part 2* (1968): 1137–1165.

CHIPPING SPARROW. 235. *Spizella passerina.* Widespread summer resident almost continental in range, except for the northern half of Canada and the far south. Winters in s. U.S., rarely northward along the coast to New York. A conspicuous though small bird of open woodland, orchard, rural roadside, town park and garden, flocking with other sparrows in winter to forage on grassy areas near cover and in weedy fields.

Favored foods include weed, grass and grain seeds, millet, cracked corn and, in summer, ants. Chippies will come readily to the ground feeder for commercial seed mixtures, crumbs, doughnuts, peanut butter mix and suet.

Nests in dense cover, 3–5 feet high, or up to 25 feet on a tree.

The eggs, four normally, are greenish-blue with brown markings. Early May–July. Incubation, 11–12 days by females; fledging, 12 days. Two broods.

Read: Bent, A. C., *Bulletin 237, Part 2* (1968): 1166–1186.

FIELD SPARROW. 236. *Spizella pusilla.* A common bird of brushy and neglected fields and meadows from s. Quebec through the northern states west to Minnesota, south to the northern parts of the Gulf states. Winters in s. U.S., less common northward to New York and Illinois.

The Field Sparrow is a ground-feeding *spizella* with much the same food habits and preferences as the previous species. It will partake of all the same foods at the bird table.

Nest, in a clump of grass, tangle or thicket, often in a blackberry or multiflora rose.

Eggs, 3–5 pale green, marked with red. Incubation, 11 days by female; fledging, 11–14 days. Two broods.

Read: Bent, A. C., *Bulletin 237, Part 2* (1968): 1217–1236.

HARRIS' SPARROW. 236. *Zonotrichia querula.* Our largest sparrow breeds in the dwarf spruce habitat bordering the tundra of w. Canada. It migrates through the prairie states and winters in a restricted area from s. Nebraska to Texas. Occasionally wanders eastward in autumn.

In winter it is a bird of the brushy roadside, riverbottom and clearings in open woodlands. Its food, which it gleans by vigorous scratching of the ground, includes many weed and grass seeds, grain, sunflower seeds and berries. Prefers to feed on the ground, but will come to the well-stocked bird table.

Read: Bent, A. C., *Bulletin 237, Part 3* (1968): 1249–1273.

WHITE-CROWNED SPARROW. 237. *Zonotrichia leucophrys.* Breeds in the far north along dwarf willow edges of water, winters mostly west of the Appalachians from mid-U.S. latitudes south to Georgia, Louisiana and Texas.

In winter months it is a bird of grassy borders, woodland edges, brushy fields, often in mixed sparrow flocks. It feeds on all the field weed and grain seeds, and will come to the feeder (ground-strewn largess) for commercial seed mixtures, crumbs, sunflower seeds, nutmeats and raisins.

Read: Blanchard, B. D., The White-crowned Sparrow of the Pacific Seaboard," *University of California Publications in Zoology 46* (1941): 1–178. (Berkeley, California). Bent, A. C., *Bulletin 237, Part 3* (1968): 1273–1352.

WHITE-THROATED SPARROW. 237. *Zonotrichia albicollis.* Likes conifer forests for breeding, especially spruce. Range is from mid-Provinces south into the mountains of New York, Pennsylvania, and central Minnesota. Winters from the northern states south to the Gulf.

A bird of woodland, park, field and garden, and often one of the most regular patrons of the feeding station.

The White-throat's menu includes a vast variety of berries, seeds, grains, and in summer, arthropod and other invertebrate food. Like the other sparrows, it prefers to feed on the ground and will consume everything from bread crumbs to cracked corn.

Nest is in a concealed location on the ground in woodland or forest.

Eggs, 3–5, are pale green spotted with brown. Early May–August. Incubation, 12–14 days; fledging, 14 days. One brood.

Read: Bent, A. C., *Bulletin 237, Part 3* (1968): 1364–1392.

Fox Sparrow. 237. *Passerella iliaca.* Breeds in our area almost exclusively in Canada in wet woodlands from Labrador and Maritime provinces throughout the southern half of Canada. Winters in the U.S. north to s. Illinois and New York.

A bird of forest clearing and edge, it is found in winter in thicket and tangle and sheltered bottomland. Its natural food is largely berries and seeds (arthropods in summer) like other sparrows, except that it favors berries of all types to a greater extent. Scatter its favorite foods on the ground near cover.

Nests on or near the ground in a tangle or in underbrush.

Eggs, four, pale green spotted with reddish brown. June–July. Incubation, 12–14 days; fledging, 12–14 days. One or two broods.

Read: Bent, A. C., *Bulletin 237, Part 3* (1968): 1392–1434.

Song Sparrow. 239. *Melospiza melodia.* Abundant and ubiquitous bird throughout the book area from mid-Canada latitudes (in summer) southward, wintering commonly throughout the U.S., but migrating from northern areas.

A bird of field and marsh, woodland and park, thicket and garden, farm and suburb.

Grass and weed seeds are the principal diet; the Song Sparrows in your garden will be regular feeders on all the small seeds you scatter on the ground or set on your feeding trays.

The nest is on the ground or near it in clumps or grass or weeds or in dense shrubbery.

The eggs, 3–5, are greenish-white marked with brown. April–August. Incubation, 12–13 days by female; fledging, 10 days. Two or three broods.

Read: Nice, M. M., "Studies in the Life History of the Song

Sparrow," *Transactions of the Linnaean Society of New York 4* (1937): 1–227; *6* (1943): 1–328. (Available in reprint: New York: Dover Press.) Bent, A. C., *Bulletin 237, Part 3* (1968): 1491–1564.

INTRODUCED SPECIES OF VERY LOCAL DISTRIBUTION.

RED-WHISKERED BULBUL. *Pycnonotus jocosus.* Locally common around South Miami, Florida, where it was introduced from India in 1955.

Feeds predominantly on insects and berries. Will come to the bird bath, and is attracted by plantings of berry-bearing shrubs.

SPOT-BREASTED ORIOLE. *Icterus pectoralis.* Central American native, now established in Dade County, Florida.

Will come to the bird feeder for avocado, banana, bread, oranges and berries. Attracted by the bird bath.

EUROPEAN TREE SPARROW. 209. *Passer montanus.* A weaver like the House Sparrow but more rural in habitat preference. Introduced from Europe and now established around St. Louis, Missouri and northward into Calhoun and St. Clair counties, Illinois.

Feeds on corn, oats, wheat, insects.

Nests generally in the same sites as House Sparrows, and will occupy bluebird-sized boxes.

Eggs, 4–6, variable, grayish-brown with darker stipplings. Late April–May. Incubation, 12–14 days by both sexes; fledging, 12–14 days. Two broods, sometimes three.

Appendices

A. Recipes

1. BASIC PUD

Take seeds, peanuts, cheese, oatmeal, dry cake and scraps. Put them in a container, pour hot fat (melted suet) over the mixture until it is covered, and leave to set. Turn out onto a plate, unless you have prepared it in a coconut shell; hang from tree or table. Rough quantities: one pound of mixture to ½-pound of melted fat. Any bell-shaded, cup-shaped or even empty tin can container will do.

2. BIRD CAKE

Mix 2 lbs. self-raising flour, ½-pound margarine and a little sugar with water and bake like a large bun.

3. ANTI-SPARROW PUDDING

Boil together for five minutes one cup of sugar and one cup of water. Mix with one cup of melted suet, bacon fat or shortening and leave to cool. Mix with breadcrumbs, bird seed, a little boiled rice and scraps, until the mixture is very stiff. Then pack it into any kind of tin can or glass jar. Lay the can on its side in a tree or on the window sill or in any place where birds can perch and pick out the food.

4. MEALWORM CULTURE

Prepare a large circular pie tin as follows: punch small holes in the lid for ventilation. Place a layer of old burlap in the bottom, and sprinkle fairly thickly with bran. Put in a slice or two of bread, raw potato, followed by two more layers of burlap/bran/bread/potato, like a three-decker sandwich. You can put a raw cabbage leaf on top, if you like. Keep the tin at room temperature, not in the hot sun.

Now introduce two or three hundred mealworms (buy them at a pet shop) into the prepared tin. After a few weeks the mealworms will turn into creamy pupae, then into little black beetles. The beetles will lay eggs, which will hatch into mealworms, and so on. Crop as necessary. Replace bread, potato and cabbage as needed. If you want to start new colonies, prepare another tin and transfer some bits of dry bread with beetle eggs from the flourishing colony.

B. Suppliers

The list below is clearly incomplete, there being literally hundreds of suppliers of feeders, food, nestboxes, optical equipment and bird bath equipment for birds. In our home area, a New York suburb, every garden supply store sells them, and most supermarkets sell seeds. Listing does not imply endorsement of company or product.

Equipment—General

Ardsley Woodcraft Products, Inc., 263 Douglas Road, Staten Island, N.Y. Feeders, poles, suet cakes.

Ben Smith Martin Houses, Bailey's Harbor, Wisconsin, 40202. Martin and other bird houses.

Beverly Specialties Co., Box 9, Riverside, Illinois. Bird bath sprays.

Bird Furniture, Box 781, Torrington, Connecticut, 06790. Suet feeder.

Bower Manufacturing Co., Inc. 1021 South 10-F, Goshen, Indiana. Glass hopper feeder.

Colebrook Specialties, Colebrook, Connecticut, 06790. Hopper feeder.

Dorbud Products, 6855 Van Nuys Blvd., Van Nuys, California, 91405. Hummingbird feeder.

Duncraft, Dunn Building, Penacook, New Hampshire, 03301. Feeders, mesh suet bags, houses. Complete supply house.

Hyde Bird Feeder Co., 56 Felton St., Waltham, Massachusetts. Trip-perch feeder.

Hummingbird Heaven, 6618A Apperson Street, Tujunga, California, 91042. Hummingbird feeder, oriole feeder.

Massachusetts Audubon Society, 155 Newberry Street, Boston, Massachusetts. Complete service department for bird garden and bird watcher. Books. Free catalog.

Smith-Gates Corp., Farmington, Connecticut. Water warmer.

Songbirds, East Woodstock, Connecticut 06244. Pipe fittings, valves for bird bath.

Tucker Wild Bird Sanctuary, 29322A Modjeska Canyon Road, Orange, California, 92667. Hummingbird feeder.

Valley Bird Shoppe, 4870 Lander Road, Chagrin Falls, Ohio, 44022. Weathervane feeder.

Wildlife Refuge, East Lansing, Michigan. Large capacity hopper feeder.

Woodland Specialties, Box 395, Hempstead, New York 11951. Feeders.

Yield House, North Conway, New Hampshire 03860. Martin house kits.

SEEDS

Hinton & Co., 1160 Myrtle Avenue, Brooklyn, New York. Write for price list. Wild bird seeds.

Pecano Bird Feed Company, 110 West Street, Albany, Georgia. Write for price list. Wild bird seeds.

Prunty Seed & Grain Co., 620 North Second Street, St. Louis, Missouri, 63102. Seeds, seed mixes. Write for quotation.

C. Birds which visit feeding stations

The following waterfowl (and occasionally some others) will come to scattered corn and grain in or adjacent to a suitable pond.

Mute Swan
Canada Goose
Mallard
Black Duck
Gadwall
Pintail
Green-winged Teal
Blue-winged Teal
Shoveler
American Widgeon
American Coot

The birds listed below will come to the ground, elevated bird table, special feeder or bird bath when suitably provisioned.

Bobwhite
Rock Dove (Common Pigeon)
Ring-necked Pheasant
Mourning Dove
Ground Dove
Ruby-throated Hummingbird
Rufous Hummingbird*
Yellow-shafted Flicker
Red-shafted Flicker
Pileated Woodpecker
Red-bellied Woodpecker
Red-headed Woodpecker
Yellow-bellied Sapsucker
Hairy Woodpecker
Downy Woodpecker
Gray Jay
Blue Jay
Scrub Jay
Black-capped Chickadee

Carolina Chickadee
Boreal Chickadee
Tufted Titmouse
White-breasted Nuthatch
Red-breasted Nuthatch
Brown-headed Nuthatch
Brown Creeper
Carolina Wren
Mockingbird
Catbird
Brown Thrasher
Robin
Wood Thrush
Hermit Thrush
Eastern Bluebird
Golden-crowned Kinglet
Bohemian Waxwing*
Cedar Waxwing
Starling

Myrtle Warbler
Pine Warbler
House Sparrow
European Tree Sparrow*
Eastern Meadowlark
Western Meadowlark
Red-winged Blackbird
Orchard Oriole
Spot-breasted Oriole*
Baltimore Oriole
Boat-tailed Grackle
Common Grackle
Brown-headed Cowbird
Cardinal
Black-headed Grosbeak
Blue Grosbeak
Indigo Bunting
Painted Bunting*
Dickcissel
Evening Grosbeak

Purple Finch
House Finch
Pine Grosbeak
Common Redpoll
Pine Siskin
American Goldfinch
Rufous-sided Towhee
Slate-colored Junco
Oregon Junco*
Tree Sparrow
Chipping Sparrow
Field Sparrow
Harris' Sparrow
White-crowned Sparrow
White-throated Sparrow
Fox Sparrow
Song Sparrow

* Rare or local in our area.

Many other species may be attracted to water occasionally (especially in motion from a drip or spray) during migration or during drought periods, including thrushes, warblers, etc.

The following species may frequent the bird garden as predators.

Goshawk
Sharp-shinned Hawk
Cooper's Hawk
Sparrow Hawk
Northern Shrike
Loggerhead Shrike

Barn Owl
Screech Owl
Great Horned Owl
Long-eared Owl
Saw-whet Owl

D. Birds which use nestboxes

Wood Duck
Common Goldeneye*
Hooded Merganser
Common Merganser
Sparrow Hawk
Barn Owl
Screech Owl
Saw-whet Owl
Yellow-shafted Flicker
Red-shafted Flicker
Red-bellied Woodpecker
Red-headed Woodpecker
Hairy Woodpecker
Downy Woodpecker
Great Crested Flycatcher
Eastern Phoebe
Tree Swallow

Purple Martin
Black-capped Chickadee
Carolina Chickadee
Boreal Chickadee
Tufted Titmouse
White-breasted Nuthatch
Red-breasted Nuthatch
House Wren
Winter Wren*
Bewick's Wren
Carolina Wren
Eastern Bluebird
Starling
Prothonotary Warbler*
House Sparrow
European Tree Sparrow
* Very rarely

The following species sometimes nest on or about man-made structures.

Osprey (telephone poles or special platforms)
Common Nighthawk (rooftops)
Chimney Swift (chimneys, barns)
Barn Swallow (eaves, outbuildings, boat houses)
Cliff Swallow (eaves, sides of barns)
House Finch (crannies around houses)

E. Treatment of casualties

1. ORPHANED OR EXHAUSTED BIRDS

First of all, be sure the bird is really in need of help. Young birds of some species flutter from the nest before they are really able to fly and wind up in the underbrush or under hedges waiting to be fed. Sometimes they are silent; sometimes they chirp. Often you will hear the nearby parent bird "talking" to the errant youngster. This is perfectly normal, and the birds should be left alone. Every year thousands of young Robins, Blue Jays, Catbirds and others are "rescued" before they are lost, usually by small children. Often the rescues prove fatal.

Young birds that are in a state of development that indicates that they have fallen from the nest require special handling. If the nest is accessible, you should gently and carefully return the bird to it. If this is not possible, or if a young bird almost ready to fly is not being attended or is in imminent danger from a predator, you may decide to act as a foster parent. Be advised that this is a time-consuming and demanding job, albeit rewarding if successful.

Your first task, especially if the bird is very young, is to provide a substitute nest. A fruit box lined with crumpled facial tissues, or any small cardboard box with a soft lining will suffice. Suit the box to the size of the bird—obviously a young crow needs a larger box than a young vireo. Keep the box warm, dry, clean and draft-free. It should never be placed in direct sunlight. In order to insure that a growing bird has body support (to help the legs grow straight), objects similar in size to nestling birds may be placed around your youngster. Rolled up cotton socks, for example.

Feeding very young birds is a never-ending chore, since during this period of their development growth is very rapid and food demand is almost constant. Every twenty minutes is ideal; one filling per hour is the minimum. Parent birds are busy from dawn to dark bringing food to the nest. You are their surrogate.

Various types of food for rearing very young birds have been recommended. Some experts suggest soft-bodied insects such as caterpillars which you have first killed. Other experts prefer at first to feed finely chopped egg yolk, finely minced raw hamburger meat or canned dog food, or a concoction of equal parts dry baby cereal and hard-cooked egg yolk, moistened and thoroughly blended with raw egg white or milk, with cod liver oil (one drop) used occasionally with the moistening fluid. Bread crumbs soaked in milk may be used in an emergency.

As the young bird develops, the menu can be broadened to include (for insect eaters—and remember that most seedeaters feed insects to their nestlings) finely minced hamburger or dog food, finely chopped greens, bits of charcoal, gravel and crushed seeds. Other food for growing birds would include insects, mealworms (available from most pet shops or bait shops or grow your own), soft fruits and berries. Do not force liquids on your little bird; you are likely to drown it. The water is in the food itself. Older birds will drink from a container placed in the cage.

It is difficult to overfeed a young bird, and it will tell you in no uncertain terms when it is hungry. Sometimes, however, it is difficult to get a very young bird to gape its bill to receive food; it needs a proper stimulus. A trick that we have found to work is to advance towards the young bird with the morsel of food impaled on a toothpick held between two crossed thumbs, with fingers of both hands flapping like wings (see the illustration on page 105). Most young birds will react instinctively and open wide to receive your offering.

Keep the cage clean and dispose of the droppings promptly. Talk to your youngster whenever you feed it, using the same words each time. When it can fly, it will come to your hand when you call it.

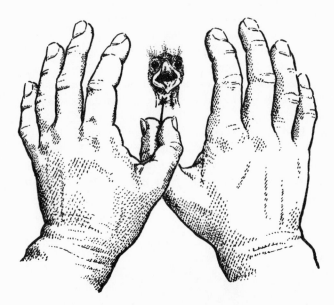

When it can fly, you should begin to prepare it for life in the wild. It is against the law to keep native American wild birds in cages unless you have a special permit. Some ornithologists believe that a young bird can be trained to forage for itself by taking it into the garden and "planting" caterpillars and letting it discover them with you. Perhaps a better system would be to begin by feeding the youngster outdoors from a pan on the ground, then from the ground itself, while gradually decreasing the food supplied. However, a hand-raised bird, untrained in foraging or insect-hawking for itself, and perhaps less alert to the dangers of the wild, is a poor survival risk at best.

2. Sick or Injured Birds

An adult bird is certainly in need of help if you can pick it up. An exhausted, sick or starving bird should be put into a box with a carpet of newpaper and a perch stick near—but not on—the floor. Give it a shallow bowl of water and a shallow dish of food. Milk-soaked bread crumbs, bits of hamburger or canned dog food or chopped hard-cooked egg yolks may be tried.

If the bird shows no interest in food, leave it to rest, but be sure it is warm. An electric light bulb near the box will provide the necessary warmth. Sleep and warmth (about 70°) are the best healers. If the bird seems to be suffering from a respiratory infection and has difficulty breathing, you might try a few drops of water (from an eye-dropper) into which an antibiotic caged-bird pill (from your pet store) has been pulverized, according to the maker's directions. It may occur to you that a few drops of whiskey in water will revive a cold and shivering bird. It will not. *Feed it no alcohol.*

If the bird is still alive after its night's sleep, it may be more interested in food or water, or it may be lively enough to be released. But no matter how we fuss over them, many sick and injured birds die in our care; perhaps from illness, perhaps from old age.

If a bird is found or brought to you bleeding or otherwise injured, it should be taken to the nearest veterinarian. Only if you are prevented by some inexorable reason from taking this course should you attempt to treat the bird yourself. But if you must, a bleeding bird should be carefully and gently examined to determine the site of the wound, which should then be treated exactly as you would treat a wound on your own body: cleansing, disinfecting, and if need be, sewing. If a wing is broken in an obvious place, it should be immobilized with a section of stocking or cellophane tape for a few days, disinfected at the break (with sulfa dust), then the bird should be allowed to move the wing, preen it and exercise it. If a leg is broken, it should be disinfected, carefully set and splinted with a toothpick, goosequill or matchstick and tape.

3. OILED BIRDS

You are not likely to find an oiled seabird in your garden, but should one be brought to you from a nearby beach, the best you can do for it is clean it gently with a very mild detergent, rinse carefully with clean water, and dust with cornstarch when semi-dry. Do not clean with gasoline, carbon-tetrachloride or other "cleaning fluids." Keep the bird warm and dry, and give it sardines, smelts or slivers of raw liver and plenty of drinking water. It will take many days before the bird's plumage returns to its waterproof state, so merely to clean it and return it to the nearest body of water will probably cause the bird to drown. Or die of exposure.

Warning! You can lose an eye by getting too familiar with such rapier-billed birds as green and night herons. They can strike out with lightning speed—faster than you can react. So keep them securely caged when treating them, and let no children handle or release them.

Further warning: Don't pick up or handle sick pigeons, Starlings or House Sparrows, as these species (especially the pigeon) are carriers of a highly communicable fungus disease.

Read: Tottenham, Katharine, *Bird Doctor*, (London: Nelson).

Lake, F. B., *Treatment of Sick and Wounded Birds,* Hertfordshire: British Trust for Ornithology (Beech Grove, Tring). Twenty-five cents should cover the cost of pamphlet and postage. Pet shops and libraries have many other books on the care of caged birds, which give much information applicable to wild birds. *Hand-taming Wild Birds at the Feeder* by Alfred G. Martin, published by Bond Wheelwright and Bantam Books, is an enthralling account of how to go about getting wild songbirds to eat out of your hand. It contains many helpful hints on care and feeding of sick or injured birds.

F. Organizations concerned with bird life

In every state and province, in most cities and in many smaller communities you will find groups of people who are actively concerned with bird life, its study and protection. (New York State alone has over 40 such organizations!) Some are local or regional bird clubs, nature study or conservation societies, some are autonomous and others branches of national organizations. Without exception they welcome new members and are always happy to advise and help the inexperienced.

Here are the more important national organizations:

National Audubon Society, 1130 Fifth Avenue, New York, N.Y., 10028. Maintains wildlife sanctuaries throughout the United States, engages in wildlife research, particularly of threatened species, maintains Audubon camps and nature centers for study and for teacher training. Its Nature Centers Division is a planning and consultant service to community wildlife and conservation centers. It publishes *Audubon* magazine bimonthly and *Audubon Field Notes* bimonthly, as well as research monographs, wildlife films, conservation and leader's guides and other visual aids. There is a vast Junior Club program, which has introduced millions of children to the world of birds. Local branches or affiliated societies—and the various relationships are complex—now number over 300. Some of the most active of these publish their own journals, maintain their own sanctuaries, and in the case of the Florida Audubon Society, conduct far-ranging field trips in Latin America.

American Ornithologists' Union. The national organization for the serious bird student. Publishes the prestigious quarterly, *The*

Auk, as well as scientific monographs, the *Check-list of North American Birds,* and is in the process of publishing the scholarly and badly-needed *Handbook of North American Birds.* The A.O.U. meets annually in a different city in the U.S. or Canada in late spring or late summer. It is concerned with bird protection as well as research. For membership write the Treasurer, currently Burt L. Munroe, Jr., Dept of Biology, University of Louisville, Louisville, Kentucky 40208.

Wilson Ornithological Society began as a regional society concerned with the birds of the Midwest, but is now nationwide in membership and scope. It publishes the highly-respected *Wilson Bulletin,* a quarterly, and meets annually, usually in early spring. The society maintains, at the University of Michigan, Ann Arbor, the Josselyn Van Tyne Memorial Library, for the use of its members. For membership information, the current Treasurer is William A. Klamm, 2140 Lewis Drive, Lakewood, Ohio, 44107.

While it is devoted primarily to the birds of the Pacific states and Central America, the Cooper Ornithological Society has many members from other parts of the continent and the world. It publishes a quarterly, *The Condor,* highly regarded in ornithological circles. Its annual meetings have always been in a western city, usually in spring, but it also conducts a regular schedule of local meetings at its two divisions, the Northern at Berkeley, and the Southern at Los Angeles.

A number of regional organizations for bird banders exist; one does not need to be a bander to enjoy the excellent journal *Bird Banding,* published by the Northeastern Bird Banding Association, also a quarterly. Its editor is E. Alexander Bergstrom, 37 Old Brook Road, West Hartford, Connecticut. The Eastern Bird Banding Association publishes *EBBA News* bimonthly. Its editor if Frank P. Frazier, 424 Highland Avenue, Upper Montclair, New Jersey. The Inland Bird Banding Association publishes *IBBA NEWS,* also bimonthly. It is edited by Terrence N. Ingram, Apple River, Illinois. Each of these groups holds annual meetings.

There are, of course, a host of national and international organizations concerned with bird protection, conservation and management. Among them are:

Wildlife Management Institute, 709 Wire Building, Washington, D.C., 20005.

Izaak Walton League, 1316 Waukegan Road, Glenview, Illinois.
National Wildlife Federation, 1412 Sixteenth Street, N.W.
Washington, D.C., 20036.

The Wildlife Society, 3900 Wisconsin Avenue, Washington, D.C.,
20016.

The World Wildlife Fund, 1816 Jefferson Place, Washington, D.C.
Nature Conservancy, 2039 K Street, Washington, D.C.

Wilderness Society, 729 15th Street, N.W. Washington, D.C.

The Sierra Club, Mills Tower, San Francisco, California; New
York, N.Y.

International Council for Bird Protection, American Branch,
American Museum of Natural History, New York, N.Y. 10024.
In Canada

Federation of Ontario Naturalists, Don Mills, Ontario, conducts
a broad program of educational activities ranging from its maga-
zines *Ontario Naturalist* and *The Young Naturalist* to its *Sounds
of Nature* recordings, the dissemination of nature news through
radio, newspaper and television; an F.O.N. camp, field gatherings
and workshop weekends.

G. Birds and the law

Since the turn of the century, the protection of the continent's
wild life has been an ever-growing concern, manifest in treaties
between nations, in national, state, province and local regulation.
An increasing body of laws and ordinances on all governmental
levels now afford protection to the great majority of the 775 species
of birds north of Mexico.

On the national level, migratory birds of many species are pro-
tected by the provisions of two conventions, one between the United
States and Great Britain, signed on August 16, 1916, relative to
the protection of birds that migrate between Canada and the
United States. On February 7, 1936, a similar convention between
Mexico and the United States was signed in Mexico City.

The Migratory Bird Treaty Act of July 3, 1918 also empowered
the Secretary of the Interior of the United States to adopt annual
hunting regulations by regions and states; it established a closed
hunting season on all songbirds, prohibited traffic in any wild
migratory birds, and set up regulations for the trapping, collecting,

keeping or exhibiting of wild birds for scientific or educational purposes.

In addition, there have been many laws enacted broadening the control of hunting of many species. The Bald Eagle Act of 1940 is one example.

States and provinces have also enacted legislation in support of federal laws, often increasing the list of protected species. The laws vary in each, but today only a very few species remain totally unprotected. Those species with the least protection generally are the three Accipitrine hawks: Goshawk, Cooper's Hawk and Sharp-shinned Hawk, the Great Horned Owl, Common Crow, Starling and House Sparrow.

Local governmental bodies are empowered to pass ordinances and local laws which can strengthen, but not weaken, the laws of higher bodies. New York City, for example, allows no hunting of any kind at any time of the year within its governmental boundaries. Many smaller communities have set themselves up as wildlife sanctuaries wherein every species is protected.

There are also Federal laws pertaining to the importation of wild birds or their feathers from foreign lands, the collecting of wild hawks for falconry, even for the possession of the bodies of wild birds found dead. In most instances, special permits are required from the local office of the Bureau of Sport Fisheries and Wildlife.

Read: *Birds in Our Lives,* U.S. Department of the Interior, (1966): 468–475.

H. Bird song recordings

With techniques and technical equipment improving, and the list of good bird song recordings constantly growing, today's bird student has a resource for study and enjoyment all but unknown a quarter of a century ago. (It is possible to use tapes or records of bird songs to attract birds to your garden, and to lure a shy songbird—whose song you recognize—to come closer to investigate its competition.)

All records listed below are 33⅓ rpm:

Common Bird Songs. Donald A. Borror. Dover Press, 1968.

A manual with 12-inch lp record.

Songbirds of America. Cornell Laboratory of Ornithology. Houghton Mifflin, Boston.

Best known garden birds. 10-inch lp.

A Field Guide to Bird Songs. Cornell Laboratory of Ornithology. Houghton Mifflin, Boston.

Over 300 bird songs, keyed to Peterson's *Field Guide.* Two 12-inch lps.

Warblers: Songs of Warblers of Eastern North America. Federation of Ontario Naturalists, Don Mills, Ontario.

400 songs of 38 species. 12-inch lp.

Finches: Songs of Fringillidae of Eastern and Central North America.

Federation of Ontario Naturalists, Don Mills, Ontario.

400 songs of 43 species. 12-inch lp.

Birds on a May Morning. Audubon Society of Rhode Island. The Droll Yankees, Providence, R.I.

36 species. 12-inch lp.

Birds of the Forest and

A Day in Algonquin Park, two of the many records produced by the Federation of Ontario Naturalists with the Canadian Broadcasting System.

Birds from the Great Plains to the Atlantic. (2 volumes.)

Ficker Records, Old Greenwich, Connecticut, who have other titles.

The Cornell Laboratory of Ornithology has a list of about 25 titles, not all of birds; most are issued by Houghton Mifflin.

I. Bird songs indoors

There's nothing more pleasurable than filling your house with bird song when all your windows must be closed. Happily, there's no great difficulty or expense to it, especially if you already own hi-fi equipment. If not, you will need an amplifier and a loud-speaker, plus a fairly good (meaning sensitive) non-directional microphone, the required length of acoustical cable, and a jack that plugs into your amplifier. (Most of them have sockets that take microphones.) Hi-fi equipment varies widely in quality and price, and the choice depends on your auditory needs and your means, but the microphone and cable can be found in any good audio-equipment store for under $20. There are also advertised, at under $30, directional (eavesdropper) mikes of extreme sensitivity that are centered in parabolic acoustical reflectors. These can pull in the songs of small birds from 100 yards or more, but they must be accurately aimed and are more suitable for recording than gathering the songs of your garden.

With your microphone placed in a tree near your bird table or water source and sheltered from the rain, you will truly bring your outdoors inside. You will hear the songs and calls not only of the birds you expect, but especially during spring migration, discover the presence of many unexpected visitors, as well as avian passersby overhead.

Many refinements to the basic system are possible. By attaching an outside speaker to your record player, you can broadcast your bird recordings or tapes and often attract inquisitive birds to your garden. With your outdoor microphone and a tape recorder, you can tape the summer sounds of your own garden, to warm you during the winter months. Or, with a timing device, you can set your equipment to awaken you at an appointed hour to the sounds of singing birds. In these days when more and more houses are air-conditioned and sealed against the songs of birds, your garden microphone will bring you back outdoors.

Bibliography

Accompanying the species list (pages 58–96) are suggested readings which you may wish to pursue for more thorough knowledge. In each case the best extant treatments are recommended, except for those that are extremely difficult to come by. (Your nearest big university or museum library should have all or most of them.)

It is not a sign of laziness on our part that so many readings are from the series of Life Histories by Arthur Cleveland Bent, issued by the U.S. National Museum and now reprinted inexpensively by Dover Press, New York. This is by far the most comprehensive work on North American birds yet published, and most more recent authors mine its 21 volumes for information. Where no reading reference is included, the reader is referred to one of the better regional books listed below:

Birds, general

Allen, Arthur A. *The Book of Birdlife*. New York: D. Van Nostrand Co., 1930.

Fisher, James, and Peterson, R. T. *The World of Birds*. New York: Doubleday & Co., 1964.

Grosvenor, Gilbert, and Wetmore, A. *The Book of Birds*. Washington, D.C.: National Geographic Society, 1937.

Peterson, Roger T. *The Birds*. New York: Life Nature Library, Time, Inc., 1963.

Rand, Austin L. *Ornithology, an Introduction*. New York: Norton, 1968.

Stefferud, Alfred, ed. *Birds in Our Lives*. Washington, D.C.: U.S. Department of the Interior, 1966.

Welty, Joel. *The Life of Birds*. New York: Knopf, 1963.

Bird watching

Fisher, James. *Watching Birds*. London: Pelican Books, 1941; rev. 1953.

Hickey, Joseph J. *A Guide to Bird Watching*. New York: Oxford University Press, 1943.

Bird biology (textbooks, some more advanced)

Lanyon, Wesley E. *Biology of Birds*. New York: Doubleday & Co., 1964.

Marshall, Alexander J., ed. *Biology and Comparative Physiology of Birds, 1,2*. Academic Press, 1960, 1961.

Pettingill, Olin S., Jr. *Ornithology in Laboratory and Field*. 4th ed. Minneapolis: Burgess Publishing Co., 1970.

Van Tyne, Josselyn, and Berger, A. *Fundamentals of Ornithology*. New York: John Wiley & Sons, 1959.

Wallace, George J. *Introduction to Ornithology*. New York: Macmillan Co., 1955.

Specialized subjects

Armstrong, Edward A. *Bird Display and Behavior*. London: Linsay Drummond, 1947. *A Study of Bird Song*. London: Oxford, 1963.

Dorst, Jean. *The Migration of Birds*. Boston: Houghton Mifflin Co., 1963.

Howard, E. *Territory in Bird Life*. London: Collins, 1948.

Saunders, Aretas A. *A Guide to Bird Songs*. New York: Doubleday & Co., 1959.

Storer, John H. *The Flight of Birds.* Bloomfield Hills: Cranbrook Institute of Science, 1948.

Identification

Alexander, W. B. *Birds of the Ocean.* New York: G. P. Putnam Sons, 1954.

Chapman, Frank. *Handbook of Birds of Eastern North America.* 2nd ed. New York: Dover Publications, Inc., 1940. ed. New York: D. Appleton & Co. (In Dover reprint)

Peterson, Roger T. *A Field Guide to the Birds.* Boston: Houghton Mifflin Co., 1947.

————. *A Field Guide to Western Birds.* Boston: Houghton Mifflin Co., 1961.

Pough, Richard H. *Audubon Bird Guide. Eastern Land Birds, Water Birds.* (2 vols.) New York: Doubleday & Co., 1946, 1951.

Robbins, Chandler S., Bruun, B., Zim, H. S. *Birds of North America.* New York: Golden Press, 1966.

Scott, Peter. *A Coloured Key to the Wildfowl of the World.* New York: Chas. Scribner's Sons, 1957.

National and Regional works

Many states have state bird books. Those recommended here are the best for general reading:

Forbush, Edward H. *Birds of Massachusetts and other New England States.* Massachusetts Department of Agriculture, 1925, 1927, 1929.

————. *Natural History of American Birds of Eastern and Central North America.* Boston: Houghton Mifflin Co., 1955.

Palmer, Ralph S., ed. *Handbook of North American Birds, Vol. I.* New Haven: Yale University Press, 1962.

————. *Maine Birds.* Cambridge, Mass.: Museum of Comparative Zoology, Bulletin 102, 1949.

Pearson, T. Gilbert. *Birds of America.* New York: Garden City Publishing Co., 1936.

Roberts, Thomas S. *Birds of Minnesota.* Minneapolis: University of Minnesota, 1932, 1936.

Sprunt, Alexander, Jr. *Florida Bird Life.* New York: Coward-McCann, 1954.

Sprunt, A., Jr., and Chamberlain, E. B. *South Carolina Bird Life.* Columbia: University of South Carolina Press, 1949.

Canada

Godfrey, W. Earl. *The Birds of Canada.* Ottawa: National Museum of Canada, 1967.
Peters, H. S., and Burleigh, T. D. *The Birds of Newfoundland.* Halifax: Department of Natural Resources, 1952.
Snyder, L. L. *Arctic Birds of Canada.* Toronto: University of Toronto, 1957.
Taverner, P. A. *Birds of Canada.* Toronto: Musson Co., 1943.
Tufts, R. W. *Birds of Nova Scotia.* Halifax, Nova Scotia Museum, 1961.

Special studies

Greenewalt, Crawford H. *Hummingbirds.* New York: Doubleday & Co., 1960.
Griscom, Ludlow, and Sprunt, A., Jr. *The Warblers of North America.* New York: Devin-Adair, 1957.
Kortwright, Francis H. *The Ducks, Geese, and Swans of North America.* Washington, D.C.: American Wildlife Institute, 1943.
May, John B. *The Hawks of North America.* New York: National Audubon Society, 1935.
Stout, Gardner D., ed. *The Shorebirds of North America.* New York: Viking Press, 1967.

Attracting birds

Davison, Verne E. *Attracting Birds from the Prairies to the Atlantic.* New York: Thomas Y. Crowell Co., 1967.
Kalmbach, E. R., and McAtee, W. L. *Homes for Birds.* Washington, D.C.: U.S. Department of the Interior Bulletin 14, 1957.
Lemmon, Robert S. *How to Attract the Birds.* New York: Doubleday & Co., 1947.
Martin, Alfred G. *Hand-taming Wild Birds at the Feeder.* Bond Wheelwright-Bantam Books, 1963.

McElroy, Thomas P. *The New Handbook of Attracting Birds.* New York: Knopf, 1961.

McKenny, Margaret. *Birds in the Garden and How to Attract Them.* Minneapolis: University of Minnesota Press, 1939.

Terres, John J. *Songbirds in Your Garden.* New York: Thomas Y. Crowell Co., 1953.

Nests

Headstrom, Richard. *Birds' Nests, a Field Guide.* New York: Ives Washburn, 1949.

Conservation

Gabrielson, Ira N. *Wildlife Conservation.* New York: Macmillan Co., 1959.

Mattheissen, Peter. *Wildlife in America.* New York: Viking Press, 1959.

Index

Index